Cowley Publications is a ministry of the brothers of the Society of Saint John the Evangelist, a monastic order in the Episcopal Church. Our mission is to provide books and resources for those seeking spiritual and theological formation. Cowley Publications is committed to developing a new generation of writers and teachers who will encourage people to think and pray in new ways about spirituality, reconciliation, and the future.

T0119838

Always Open

Being an Anglican Today

Richard Giles

Cowley Publications
Cambridge, Massachusetts

Originally published in English under the title
How to Be an Anglican
By the Canterbury Press Norwich of
St. Mary's Works, St. Mary's Plain,
Norwich, Norfolk, NR3 3BH, U.K.

Library of Congress Cataloging-in-Publication Data

Giles, Richard, 1940–
    [How to be an Anglican] Always open : being an Anglican today / Richard Giles.
        p. cm.
    Originally published: How to be an Anglican. Norwich : Canterbury Press, 2003.
    Includes bibliographical references.
    ISBN-10: 1-56101-259-9   ISBN-13: 978-1-56101-259-6 (pbk. : alk. paper)
        1. Anglican Communion. I. Title.
BX5005.G55 2004
283—dc22

2004026649

Cover design by Gary Ragaglia

Cowley Publications
4 Brattle Street
Cambridge, Massachusetts 02138
800-225-1534 www.cowley.org

To my wife,
who has never read a word I've written,
but without whom
I would never have written a word.

"The blessed held the middle course"

Fireplace inscription, Relais St. Vincent,
Ligny-le-Chatel, Champagne

I love our church and never will I depart from it. I've been frustrated by the structures of the church, angered sometimes by her policies, and sometimes uninspired by her worship. And in spite of that, I love her, because through her the living God has made himself known to me. I love her, because her way of doing theology appeals to me, I love her, in spite of her deficiencies (no church is perfect or infallible).

She is my home and I will gladly die in her.

Archbishop George Carey
speaking at the Doors of Hope Conference of the
Wakefield Diocese, Harrogate, United Kingdom
13 September 1997

Sir Anthony Absolute (raging)

Zounds! sirrah! the lady shall be as ugly as I choose: she shall have a lump on each shoulder; she shall be as crooked as the crescent; her one eye shall roll like the bull's in Cox's Museum; she shall have a skin like a mummy, and the beard of a Jew–she shall be all this, sirrah–yet I will make you ogle her all day, and sit up all night to write sonnets on her beauty.

Richard Sheridan, *The Rivals*

Contents

Introduction
Being Rather Than Doing

As I sat in Costa's bar beside the harbor at Halki, a tiny Greek island, it was a nice surprise to find that all the holidaymakers at our table were practicing Christians of one kind or another. As we ordered a further round of metaxas we were comforted in our self-indulgence by the smile from the Orthodox parish priest at the next table. As Roman Catholics, Anglicans and Protestants around that table got into some friendly banter, it was good to think that in Greece, no Western Christian is in any position to throw his or her weight about. No one can pull rank, for the simple reason that we all fall short of the mark. As far as our friendly Orthodox priest was concerned, we were *all* beyond the pale, Pope John Paul along with Jerry Falwell.

So what exactly do our different traditions have to offer? More particularly, how could I retain my identity as an Anglican amidst this oh-so-different culture at the other end of Europe? What might Anglicans have to offer that no one else could supply; what characteristics did we have that made us distinctive, different? In many ways it was easier for the others around the table, for being *other* than Anglican meant that you belonged to a community of faith that had "opted out" of the Established Church and was thereby confident in its special role and well-rehearsed in the reasons for its distinctiveness. This applies not only to England, but also to those places to which England exported its religious quarrels, notably in the settlement of North America.

For Anglicans it has always been more difficult, for it has sometimes seemed that we are simply what is left once you have extracted all those with passions to proclaim, placards to parade, or axes to grind. When all those who are distinctive and different have gone off to the crusades, we are the ones left at home by the fireside, companionable and undemanding. We are the residual church, the bland leading the bland.

But is it really like that? Surely we have a very special, if seemingly indefinable, instinctive way of doing things that is essentially Anglican? Do we not have something to treasure, something to offer, something so typically "us" that even the glorious and incomparable liturgy of the Orthodox Church might pall after a time, and cause us to pine for evensong in a country church—wheezing harmonium, lousy sermon and all?

These notes were written with some particular friends in mind: a group of adult confirmation candidates from a variety of backgrounds—some Roman Catholics, some Pentecostal—who found themselves at home in the parish I served, and who wanted to know more about the Anglican middle way. But whoever or wherever you may be, I hope that by reading this little book you will find something of value in our Anglican approach that might encourage you to keep us company on our journey home to God. Perhaps something might even become so special to you that you would never again let it go, but guard it as lovingly as the treasure hidden in the field.

This task is not without its difficulties. First, because the Anglican Church exhibits neither hauteur or secrecy, it is the kind of institution about which everyone already knows everything there is to know, or thinks they do. It is an open book, so everyone feels entitled to become an instant expert on its strange habits.

Second, the churches of the Anglican Communion often appear to exist chiefly for the purpose of keeping God amused, and indeed that's no mean calling. It is truly a wonderful, and sometimes comical, creation; a church quite unlike any other, which defies most attempts to classify or tame it, but which is all the stronger for not taking itself too seriously. Certainly it will drive you mad at times, for it lacks the machinery necessary for enforcing the party line, and has neither the ruthlessness to expel the intruder nor the earnestness always to get off its backside as quickly as it should. If you persevere, you will become exasperated and sometimes angry. You will not find in Anglicanism a structure of cast-iron certainties bolted securely one on top of another, but neither will you have to suspend your rational thought processes upon entering our doors.

You will find in Anglican tradition a consistent, holistic approach in which faith is not holed up in a separate "religious" compartment but is part of life. It offers no safe havens or cocoons in which we can evade the piercing eyes of the same Jesus who had only to look at Peter (Luke 22:61) to say all there was to be said. Anglicanism will offer you life on the road with Jesus of Nazareth, with the same certainties and doubts experienced by his first group of followers, as they struggled to keep up with him along all those dusty miles, grappling with the puzzle of who on earth this strange and wonderful man could be.

So if you are in the mood for an adventure, and can cope with a degree of uncertainty along the way, able to enjoy the journeying as much as the arriving, then read on.

2 What's in a Name?

Perhaps the first thing to do is to have a look at this word *Anglican*. There are still many people in the Church of England—even more in the Episcopal Church[1]—who look rather surprised when you tell them they are Anglicans, and members of the Anglican Communion. *Anglican* has now come into regular use to describe all or any of the churches across the world that have sprung from the Church of England—originally in areas colonized by the British, and subsequently in other parts of the world where Britons were to be found living, trading, and getting the locals to sit in straight lines while they were told the good news that God was an Englishman.

So it is that today, you will find quaint little eccentricities, peculiar historical hangovers, popping up in various corners of the earth, all part of this weird and wonderful Anglican legacy of Englishness. Thus you can track down, should you so wish, high-tech Texans addressing God in archaic English coined centuries before their state was born, or black bishops in the remotest parts of Africa sweltering under the weight of convocation robes, white ruffs and all, designed for sixteenth-century English winters. There we go . . . keeping God amused again.

The Anglican Communion got off to a very shaky start as an international body, indicative of the weaknesses inherent in a system suspicious of centralized authority. In a staggering lack of visionary and strategic thinking (nothing changes), the English Church made no provision for episcopal oversight in the American Colonies following the settlement of Virginia in 1607. There was no concept of missionary work, and for nearly two hundred years, settlements were staffed by state chaplains working under the jurisdiction of the Bishop of London(!). It was left to Anglican bishops in Scotland to cut through the complacency and prevarication by consecrating in 1784 the first bishop to serve in the United States, Samuel Seabury.[2] Gradually thereafter the term *Anglican* came into use more and more to satisfy conflicting needs: to satisfy the growing desire for political independence, and at the same time to recall us to our common roots.

In the British Isles, a varied patchwork of Anglican activity has emerged from the turmoil of the centuries. Whereas the English Church remains Established, the Irish Church was disestablished in 1869, in a move reflecting the deepening religious and political divides in that country. The Welsh Church followed suit in 1920, in response to growing demands from Nonconformists that the privileged position of the Established Church in Wales should be brought to an end. In Scotland, Anglicanism emerged as a separate body only after the long, drawn-out battle to make the Established Church of Scotland episcopal was finally lost with the accession of William and Mary in 1689. So today we have four different churches responding to four very different situations, working closely together but administered separately: an Anglican Communion in miniature.

Further afield it made less and less sense politically for churches founded as a by-product of British colonialism, and remaining in communion with Canterbury, to be encumbered by the word *England* in their names. "The Church of England in Australia," for example, might once have been a selling point for homesick settlers hanging up their harps by a lonely billabong, but is an absolute no-no for first-generation republicans swilling down their Fosters and telling not-so-complimentary jokes about Limeys. Such a name-tag is doomed once any nation comes of age.

The reason why, in North America, the title *Anglican* was acceptable in Canada but not the United States is likewise not difficult to understand, even if the alternative chosen–*Episcopal*–is not without irony in that nowhere in the Anglican Communion will you find a church more congregational and less episcopal than the Episcopal Church in the United States. Sadly, in the U.S. today, *Anglican* is a word often hijacked by breakaway groups of ecclesial purists whose spiritual arrogance is a denial of everything the word stands for.

After the Second World War the old British Empire disintegrated apace, and many new ecclesiastical provinces were founded as former dominions and colonies strove to match political independence with autonomy in church life. At the same time there was no wish to sever the links with Canterbury or to deny our common heritage, and a growing sense of belonging to a worldwide Anglican Communion helped cement together churches in sometimes widely disparate nation states.

The stylish glossy magazine *Anglican World*–the brainchild of American Episcopalians in the 1960s and now published by the Anglican Communion Office in London–was but one example of the growing self-awareness of Anglicans worldwide. It helped enormously to instill in all those in communion with the See of Canterbury, in whatever continent they found themselves, a sense of belonging and identity and of their unique contribution to the Christian story. For Christians of English descent no longer wishing to be tied to mother's apron strings, it would be difficult to conceive of a better name than Anglican, which recalled all those of Canterbury stock to the ancient name of the English Church– *Ecclesia Anglicana*–without mentioning the dreaded E word.

The Archbishop of Canterbury, by virtue of his office as senior bishop in the Anglican Communion–first among equals–continues to exercise a particular ministry of unity, in which affection is more significant than authority. In addition, the Anglican Communion has a network of mutual support and communication in the Lambeth Conference (the consultative gathering of all Anglican bishops, which now takes place once every ten years), the regular meetings of the Primates of the Anglican Provinces, and the work of the Anglican Consultative Council. Holding together a communion of such incredible diversity and independence of spirit is sometimes a headache, but somehow we manage it.

So then, becoming an Anglican is a far far bigger and better thing than simply joining your national church, for a new member is incorporated into a worldwide federation of forty-four provinces totaling 70 million members.

And yet . . . wherever you go within the Anglican Communion, you will encounter a certain Englishness, in the instinctive approach if no longer in the name. In its interpretation of the ancient creeds, the Church of England evolved a distinctive ethos in which the words restraint, understatement and self-deprecation spring to mind, alongside beauty and dignity, excellence and unassuming godly wisdom. It values freedom and distrusts centralization. It has a distaste for extremism of any kind.

Anglicanism, wherever it is encountered, is no place for the triumphalist. On the whole it stays humble before the mysteries of God and is (somewhat too) self-effacing before humanity. The fundamentalist has an unhappy time too, for Anglicanism has little time for idolatry, whether of unerring Scripture or infallible Pope. As Bishop David Jenkins of Durham put it, "We are not papalist Roman and we are not biblicist Protestant."[3] But Anglicanism knows about reverence, and at the same time about being at home with God; about dignified and glorious worship and at the same time about maintaining a sense of proportion and a sense of humor.

And of course, Anglicanism today embraces millions of fellow pilgrims from vastly differing cultures with whom we share so rich an inheritance, and whose fresh expressions of Anglican life constantly make our story more and more worth the telling.

3 To Begin at the Beginning

Anglicanism is not a "religion," of course, (no more than Roman Catholicism or Methodism), but simply a tradition within the one Christian religion, offering a distinctive interpretation of the old faith, but nothing new. Geoffrey Fisher, Archbishop of Canterbury from 1945 to 1961, was fond of reminding us that the Church of England has no creeds of its own, only those of the One, Holy, Catholic and Apostolic Church, undivided between East and West.[1] So it is for all Anglicans.

Although *Anglican* is an adjective adopted into common usage only during the last century, to be an Anglican in England is to belong to an ancient church, *the* ancient church of that country. This gets up other people's noses somewhat, but there it is. Even Anglican self-effacement cannot stretch to despising its own birthright, although the ignorance of the media (even of the so-called quality newspapers) misleads many into believing the fable that the Church of England was an invention of Tudor times.

It was not, of course, Henry VIII who founded the Church of England, but the unknown missionary who first ran his boat onto its shores in foolhardy eagerness to share the good news of Jesus of Nazareth with the fierce tribesmen of that wild and wet island.

Perhaps even more likely, it was the unknown Roman soldier who ran the gauntlet of barrack-room abuse to admit his allegiance to a Galilean freedom-fighter executed by their emperor two hundred years before. No one knows exactly when, or by what route, the good news came, but the date of the death of the first British martyr, Alban, has been placed as early as 209. Certainly, British bishops were present at the Council of Arles in 314, so things must have been up and running by then.

In other words, the Church of England is simply the Church of the English people, the English Church, *Ecclesia Anglicana*: its title relating not to a denominational formula, but simply to a geographical delineation. Over the last seventeen centuries or so, it has undergone innumerable changes and transformations, looping the loop a few times but always returning to base.

Not surprisingly, the most traumatic changes concern our on-off relations with Rome, the mother of the Western Church of which the Church of England remains a part. Although we cut the apron strings some time ago, we never forget Mothering Sunday. Sadly, mother cannot yet bring herself to invite us back for Sunday lunch.

More than three hundred years after Christianity was brought to these islands, the Christian community here was eventually brought under the jurisdiction of Rome after the arrival in 597 of the Italian missionary-monk Augustine. Nearly a thousand years later the link was broken and restored several times in the "off and on" Tudor period—on, then off (Henry VIII), off (Edward VI), on again (Mary), then finally off (Elizabeth I). This final break was, on both sides of the dispute, political as much as theological, with those in England who sought power and wealth harnessing and manipulating to their own ends the ferment of new theological ideas then sweeping the continent.

It is almost impossible for us now to conceive what life in the fast lane must have been like in mid–sixteenth-century Tudor England. Europe was having its mind blown by the hard drug of a radical theology emanating from Germany (again nothing changes!), which renounced entirely the notion that the hierarchy of the Church could maintain the hitherto unquestioned monopoly—and a profitable one at that—in the trade between man and

God. The Church of the West—the Church centered on Rome rather than Constantinople—began to disintegrate as theologians in Germany, Switzerland, and then England exchanged ideas and egged each other on with increasing excitement at this revolution in thought, known as the Reformation, which was to change forever the face of Christian practice and worship.

It wasn't long before kings and princes cottoned on to the political potential of this cataclysmic change, realizing that it provided the opportunity for a convenient revolution of another kind—against the spiritual imperialism of the papacy and its hitman, the leader of the Habsburg dynasty, still styled rather quaintly "the Holy Roman Emperor."

In England's case, the king happened to be Henry VIII, who combined a vindictive hot temper with intense bouts of religious mania—a volatile mixture which made life for those around him a bit like a game of Russian roulette. What was orthodoxy yesterday could be heresy by the morning, and the wrong answer to the test question could result not merely in a failed paper but in a slow and agonizing death.

The theologian who came out on top at the time was Thomas Cranmer, an academic and career diplomat whose meteoric rise to the Archbishopric of Canterbury was due almost entirely to his negotiating skills on Henry's behalf in the little matter of the annulment of the king's first marriage to Catherine of Aragon, who had failed to bear him a male heir. Although Cranmer failed to deliver the goods in this instance, Henry realized that, given Cranmer's increasingly anti-Roman views (it was he who first declared the pope to be none other than the antichrist of 1 John 2:18), he would be just the man to mastermind a complete break from Rome, should diplomacy finally prove fruitless. Cranmer fit the bill perfectly because he abhorred the power vacuum created by the deletion of the Pope's name from Henry's Christmas card list, and he immediately set to work with enthusiasm to fill the gap, digging deep into his Old Testament to crank up the dubious but convenient doctrine of the anointed king. Henry, supported by Cranmer, duly appointed himself "the only supreme head in earth of the Church of England, called *Anglicana Ecclesia*."[2]

Thus it was that Henry's obsessional search for a male heir and his passionate interest in religious ideas (the Pope had declared him "Defender of the Faith" before their falling-out) were complemented perfectly in an archbishop anxious to reshape the English Church. Each seized the opportunity provided by this moment of mutual need, and pursued his own agenda. Piggy-in-the-middle was the dear old C of E, which in the process simply exchanged one form of totalitarianism for another.

Cranmer would be seen by some as a Margaret Thatcher type, in that he began sensibly enough with badly needed reforms (ending abuses, attacking superstition, translating the Bible and giving us a Mass in English) but then proceeded to lose all sense of proportion. Whereas Mrs. Thatcher wasn't European enough, Cranmer was a little too keen on Europe, especially on the hot-headed Reformers from Switzerland for whom Martin Luther was a dubious conservative.

Although in the early years after the break with Rome, conservatives and reformers were equally matched, Cranmer gradually gained the upper hand, and in a decidedly un-Anglican manner abandoned all pretense of moderation as he pressed home his advantage. He sat by while the monasteries were dissolved and the religious orders suppressed (kicking his own sister out of a job in the process[3]), and led the way in the abolition of time-honored ceremonies and the destruction of the shrines of the saints and of all images in our parish churches. The successive Prayer Books which Cranmer master-minded and enriched with his own special liturgical genius also reveal an escalating tendency to renounce the old and embrace the new, with an increasing intolerance typical of the convert.

But as we were saying, yesterday's orthodoxy was tomorrow's heresy, and when Henry's eldest daughter, Mary, ascended the throne, the pendulum swung back the other way, and Cranmer himself went to his death. It wasn't until the reign of Elizabeth I, Henry's daughter by Anne Boleyn, that some form of equilibrium was established, and a proper Anglican balance achieved between conservation and change.

This was England after all, and in the end these foreign theological ideas were not swallowed wholesale but merely allowed to trickle down the throat. Those who worked to renew and reform the Church of England in this time of upheaval were very careful to maintain continuity between old and new. Before and after the break with Rome, almost without exception, the same priests in the same parish churches continued to lead and to minister to the same communities of faith, and where new cathedrals were created from old abbeys, it was often the last abbot in the old order who became first bishop in the new. For most people, life just went on as before, and in those days–before the term *quality of life* had been invented–mere survival was considered a bonus. Despite the introduction of new liturgies in the vernacular, together with an English version of the Scriptures,[4] a sense of continuity was given by the same people gathering in the same church building, with the same old priest, albeit looking a little more harassed and careworn, perhaps now with a wife as well as a bishop to keep happy.

Despite the upheaval and, at times, distress, the sense of continuity remained undimmed. Those who faithfully made their way to the parish church each Sunday knew they belonged to the ancient Church of this land, a Church which had seen popes and princes come and go, and which would continue to be the Church of the English people, whatever anybody did or said. The Reformers recognized this and were intent on a return to the primitive Church, not the creation of a new one. They had no interest in building a new house, only in spring-cleaning the old one.[5]

A teenage crisis, not unique to our household, once saw my daughter's favorite white top come out of the washing machine looking decidedly pink. This required a dash to town and the purchase of a strong red dye to make a virtue out of necessity: hey presto, a new red top! Relief all round and domestic harmony re-established. Only it wasn't new of course. It was the same old top, every fiber of it, but given a new look. The Church of England was given a completely new look at the Reformation, but it was the same Church, fiber for fiber.

It was the conviction of those who refurbished the English Church in the sixteenth century that it was perfectly possible to be a good Catholic without submitting oneself to the bishop of

Rome. In this, Anglicans keep company with the 350 million-strong Orthodox Communion which is of the same opinion, and who in 1054 went so far as to excommunicate the Pope, just in case anyone was in any doubt about the matter. (But this excommunication was annulled in 1965, so perhaps it will take only another 900 years for us all to be good friends again.)

The Church of England is therefore a Christian body that is both Catholic (in that it prizes and enjoys an unbroken continuity[6] of Christian life and witness within the framework of an episcopal, sacramental Church), and Reformed (in that it is heir to the liberating insights of the Reformation and delights in Scripture as a life-giving resource and as the only authority essential for Christian doctrines). In this the Anglican Communion is in a unique position to serve as a "house of reconciliation" for all the churches, presenting a realistic *modus vivendi* of how Christians of different cultures and religious instincts can live together in unity. If we can do it, anyone can!

Like all great Christian traditions, Anglicanism does not simply look back to the past, resting on brown and brittle laurels like last year's Christmas wreath. It has exhibited the energy over the centuries to renew itself many times. These movements of renewal have reinvigorated the Church, often at times of spiritual torpor, by recalling it to a particular aspect of its many-faceted heritage or to a characteristic which had long lain dormant.

In the late eighteenth century for example, the Evangelical Revival,[7] led by Henry Venn, John Newton, and later Charles Simeon, sought to give a fresh vision to a Church beset by worldliness and served by a clergy prone to negligence. The Bible, and only the Bible, was the movement's touchstone, and the individual believer's heart and mind the battleground. Evangelicals were concerned above all with conversion as a recognizable moment of turning one's life over to God, an event made possible solely by the grace of God accessed through the sacrificial death of Jesus Christ. The Evangelical Revival recalled a rather frivolous Church to the serious business of living and preaching the Christian gospel, and was not always thanked for spoiling the fun with its sober earnestness. It gave a new fervor and urgency to missionary work abroad (founding the Church Missionary Society in

1799, one among many such societies springing up at that time) and to dedicated pastoral care at home (founding the Church Pastoral Aid Society in 1836). The movement reminded the Church it had serious work to do, for which the essential prerequisite was the conversion of the individual sinner through faith in the atoning death of Christ.

Since the Second World War, Evangelicals in the Church of England have emerged from the shadows to become the dominant force in the Church today, leading the way in numerical growth, lively and joyful worship, evangelistic outreach into new areas and in the number of candidates offering themselves for the ordained ministry.

Complementary to this renewal of individual hearts and minds was the renewal of the Church understood as a sacred body called into being by God. This emphasis came to be called the High Church movement, and was kept alive throughout the seventeenth century by the Caroline Divines and by the Nonjurors—the nine bishops (including the Archbishop of Canterbury) and four hundred clergy who in 1688 refused to take the Oath of Allegiance to William and Mary, and were removed from office as a result.

It was not until the 1830s, however, that the flame was fanned into a blaze. In 1833 an audacious sermon preached at Oxford by a priest-academic called John Keble was to change everything. The newly elected Whig administration of the day proposed, on grounds of economy, to suppress ten Irish bishoprics. Keble seized upon this threatened incursion by the secular power to reaffirm the nature of the Church as a holy creation of God, not a mere man-made institution.

Keble entitled his sermon, preached before the Assize Judges in the University Church, "National Apostasy," and his aim was to promote action in defense of the Church in the face of the State's encroaching powers. In a way which no doubt took the gentle Keble by surprise, the Church reacted as a giant suddenly aroused from sleep, and in the years that followed set about with gusto the task of reclaiming its sacred birthright.

The Church of England was awakened to its holy calling and vocation as the ancient Catholic Church of that country, giving a

fresh emphasis to apostolic order, ordained ministry, the sacraments, the religious life and liturgy (though not ritualism, which
was a later development). Its leading lights were, in addition to
Keble himself, Edward Pusey and John Henry Newman. Although
Newman was later to defect to Rome, the main body of the movement continued within the Church of England to enrich it with a
sense of history and of sacred commission.

The Oxford Movement was throughout a very Anglican movement, determined to find within the Prayer Book the justification
for every practice it encouraged, convinced that the Church of
England had no need to look elsewhere to establish its credentials.[8] Today the spiritual heirs of the Oxford Movement (and of
the seventeenth-century High Church movement which preceded
it) are known as the Catholic wing of the Church.[9]

Other renewal movements have followed, such as the Parish
Communion Movement, beginning before the Second World War
but flowering fully after it, which sought to establish the Eucharist
as the main Sunday service in every parish. Originally there was
a breakfast to follow, expressing the corporate life awakened by
the Eucharist properly understood, and although it is now usually
truncated to a cup of coffee, the point remains.

The Parish Communion Movement was itself a manifestation
of the wider Liturgical Movement, which had begun among
Roman Catholic communities on the continent in the early twentieth century. It recaptured the Eucharist for the people of God,
rescuing it from the sanctuary—where it had become a spectacle
to observe, the sacrament an object to adore—and making it once
again a participation by the whole people of God in a sacred meal
which made present the reality of Christ. These insights had dramatic repercussions on the architecture of churches, showing us
how the design of worship spaces can be a means of understanding who we are and where we came from as the people of God.[10]

More recently, the Charismatic Renewal Movement—or more
simply, the Renewal Movement—has recalled the Church to the
freshness of its first love for God. By an emphasis on the initial
period of Christian history described in the Acts of the Apostles,
this movement has reminded us of the direct access we have to
the life and power of God, and to the gifts and ministries inherent

in every church and made available once we ask the Spirit of God to allow us to experience them. It has also restored confidence and boldness to a Church that in many areas had become demoralized, enabling worship to become the "song of them that triumph" rather than the squawks of a Church whistling in the dark. "Arise, shine, for your light has come!" was typical of the triumphant scriptural phrases set to music in the 1960s as the Church once again woke from its slumber.

The Renewal Movement, although common to all Christian traditions, has done the Anglican Church (especially in Britain) a power of good in giving us a unity undreamed of thirty years ago. In this experience, the Spirit has made good our deficiencies by pointing out that Christian maturity lies in complementing our own insights with those of others previously scorned or neglected. In this way the movement has made good sacramental Catholics of Evangelicals, and scriptural Evangelicals of Catholics. The old labels are rapidly fading into insignificance.

This balance of influences, hard won over many centuries, has slowly and painfully equipped Anglicans to understand both sides of any argument, a virtue often derided as a vice but which seems to get a favorable mention in the Beatitudes (Matt. 5:9).

The *Via Media* is a noble calling (was Newman ever really happy after abandoning it?) and it requires nerve to stay calm when those around you are losing their heads, diving into ditches on either side of the road, unable any longer to stay on the straight path of fearless enquiry and adventurous faith.[11] Anglicans are not ashamed to embrace the middle way, for when that path is examined humbly and prayerfully, it is found to be the lonely path that Jesus trod between the conflicting categories of wonder worker and political hero.

Building Blocks
Essential Elements
of Anglicanism

Strictly and theologically speaking, the four articles of faith comprising the Lambeth Quadrilateral are the building blocks of Anglicanism. To explain briefly, the four articles of faith originating with the Episcopal Church of the United States at its Chicago Convention of 1886, and formally adopted by the Lambeth Conference of all Anglican bishops in 1888, list the Apostles' Creed, the two Sacraments of Baptism and the Eucharist, and the Historical Episcopate as the three essentials (alongside the Holy Scriptures) of a reunited Christian Church.

Right now, however, in keeping with the mood of this book, I want to stick to instinctive approaches rather than doctrinal formularies. What might these instinctive approaches be? I would suggest the following, with none to be taken in isolation but each as a necessary part of the whole.

Openness

The title of this book gives the game away. The family of Anglican provinces to which the Episcopal Church belongs is always open. Open-hearted, open to new ideas, open to thinking the unthinkable, open to the misfits, the hopeless cases, and the un-categorizable ones, open when everywhere else has finally closed.

The Anglican Communion can embrace both those for whom God is a projection of our own need for meaning, and those who think God is contained between the covers of a book, together with every describable school of thought in between. No one is turned away who is truthfully engaged in the adventure of seeking God.

Openness does not make for neat definitions or tidy procedures, and any attempt at drilling in straight lines or banishing untouchables is doomed from the outset. We are a mixed bunch, an unruly classroom, a United Nations in full session attempting to pass a resolution. But we are in there together holding on, sometimes precariously, but with dogged determination, lest we lose our grip and fall into the snapping jaws of judgmental absolutism and moral superiority.

We are always open because we know only too well our constant need of God's mercy. Cast iron certainties are inappropriate when we can never be sure how God will choose to surprise us next. It might be in a carpenter's son from a one-horse town called Nazareth, or in the stranger in need of a bed for the night, or in the person that others want to banish from the church. One can never be too sure: best to remain open, always.

Common Sense

Throughout this book we will discern again and again this very English characteristic breaking through into the closely guarded worlds of theology, doctrine and canon law, to claim for the ordinary person the treasures which would otherwise be hoarded away behind locked doors.

Anglicans demand of the theologian a ready explanation that can be applied to daily life. They are impatient of very long books without pictures, and want to see some action, some movement, some glimmer of light at the end of the tunnel. In theological matters Anglicans seek simple and solid food, and in rejecting gobbledygook render the theologians a great service in rescuing them from pomposity and a lifetime of fruitless research inapplicable to the real world.

Anglicans above all are pragmatists, followers of the Great Pragmatist of Nazareth who, in telling the story of the two sons—one of whom was full of wind and one of whom got the job done—came down heavily on the side of work rather than words (Matt. 21:28). The son commended in the story had bad manners, no theology and was moody to boot, and yet he delivered the goods. His brother, so full of good intentions and a favorite with every auntie at Christmastime, turned out to be a dud.

We Anglicans likewise are keen to know what actually works. What will help get us through this vale of tears, or just this one pig of a day, with a chance of sanity and contentment at the end? What can we get our hands on, what stays still long enough for us to navigate by, what can we taste and see? We treat those who have privileged positions in the Church with affection and respect but not with awe. We are Levellers at heart, though unlike our namesakes of the seventeenth century, we don't get excited enough to organize mutinies.

Geniality

This inability to take ourselves too seriously is part and parcel of the Anglican's genial approach to life in general. This attribute can infuriate those impatient for change, but such exasperation can be fruitful—as when, every once in a while, we give birth to a prophet to be a voice crying in the wooliness. Our prophets are not usually that wild, and they can be invited back to tea with some confidence. More often than not they are loved back into the fold (and sometimes neutralized by promotion), having in the meantime prodded the Church, not beaten it to a pulp.

The Anglican is like a man who wears a baggy suit of clothes. For all of us this is usually a more comfortable experience than wearing a size too small. The opposite of a church that is "too big for its boots," the Anglican Communion never draws itself up to its full height. It is content to slouch around in this over-large suit, living comfortably within boundaries of generous proportions. It can shift around inside them, wriggle a bit, and always seem relaxed, very much at home with itself.

As a result, the Anglican rarely has "edge." He or she is not always trying to prove an ecclesiastical point or grinding a theological axe as a means of establishing superiority. Although in England and the United States the Church is notoriously middle-class, in this respect at least it reveals itself as top-drawer. It feels no need to work at being what it is, and so is devoid of all pretentiousness. Although the individual pompous ass is far from extinct among us, as an ecclesial body we are reminiscent of the titled landowner who is amused, rather than annoyed, at being mistaken for the gardener.

Generosity

The Anglican is by instinct a generous soul. Our community is one which is reluctant to draw lines, to define, to exclude. As a result it gets itself into all kinds of scrapes with those who at times (in the media or at Convention) demand to know what the hell is going on. What is going on is that we are trying our very best to reproduce the life of Jesus of Nazareth in a diverse world-wide community entering the third millennium. If it wasn't such a holy task we would call it the devil's own job, but you know what I mean.

This generosity of spirit has led us to avoid confrontation and over-expenditure of energy on issues where change is moving inexorably forward quite naturally. For example, although the ordination of gay men (and now women) has been prevalent for a very long time, bishops have preferred not to ask too many questions, lest they be told any lies. Legislation to formalize what has been going on has therefore lagged behind. This is not orderly, nor is it ruthlessly honest, but it is a path which at least affords a good measure of dignity and recognition to those given a hard time in other mainstream churches. In this way change has come, slowly but irrevocably, and without a song and dance.

Not until 2004, that is, when the General Convention of the Episcopal Church affirmed the decision of the people of the diocese of New Hampshire to call as their new bishop a man who was openly gay and in a committed relationship. Now the fat is in the fire.

Ever since I worked college vacations in a seaside hotel in Wales, I have known that chefs tend to be prima donnas and have a tendency to throw plates, and just occasionally knives. It comes as no surprise, therefore, to find that, at least for the moment, there is much leaping about, shouting, and throwing things in the Anglican kitchen. For those who have had a dull day, or who are customarily confined to the back room, such an issue provides an irresistible temptation to make one's presence felt throughout the establishment, and they are making the most of this plate-smashing opportunity.

Coincidentally, it was also in 2004 that the Church of England made a right mess of dealing with the same issue. An openly gay priest, nominated an area bishop of a large diocese, was forced to stand down after intense pressure was brought upon him by the powers that be, reacting nervously to the threat of much knife, as well as plate, throwing. It was a shameful day for the English branch of our Communion. Unlike his American counterpart of course, the English episcopal candidate was nominated rather than elected. There is much to be said for having the will of the people behind you when you are going to break the mold.

The spirit of generosity also led the Church of England down the alley of alternative episcopal oversight for those parishes which could not accept the decision of the General Synod to ordain women. In such cases, a local bishop authorizes a Provincial Episcopal Visitor (often called, informally, a "flying bishop") to provide pastoral oversight to congregations opposed to the new rules. This seemed a very good idea at the time (not least to myself), but at base such notions arise from a cafeteria theology which lurked even in the New Testament church, where people "having itching ears, accumulate teachers to suit their own likings" (2 Tim 4:3). It is ironic that those in the United States who now clamor for a protocol as detrimental to catholic order as flying bishops are precisely the group who proclaim most vigorously their catholic credentials.

Our experience, however, is that however great the hullabaloo at the time, these things, given time, will eventually blow over as our generosity of spirit slowly gets the better of our desire to go crusading. Righteous indignation may keep us pumped up initially, but after a time we begin to feel rather silly, as we see our shining armor turn a little rusty in the rain. Even where common sense fails, the pension fund concentrates the mind wonderfully. We quietly slip away from the barricades and get back to God's work.

I recall that the house where I put together this book, on the edge of the English Lake District, was lent to me by a generous (Anglican) friend who had acquired a second home—with four bedrooms no less—out of all proportion to the needs of an individual. She simply wanted to make sure that all her friends, and their friends, could enjoy it too. Likewise the Anglican Church has been generous in its provision. There is room for everyone and their friends; Tom, Dick and Harriet are more than welcome. Anglicanism is above all hospitable. It keeps open house and rarely if ever asks to check invitation cards at the door.

It is entirely appropriate that the American parish doing most to push the envelope in modeling unconditional eucharistic hospitality is an Anglican one—St. Gregory of Nyssa, San Francisco. Here the prophetic act of Jesus of sharing meals with all and sundry, no questions asked, is retranslated for today with an architectural and theological immediacy, as we shall see in Chapter Twelve, which is a powerful sign of the Kingdom. It was always likely to be an Anglican community that dared to reverse the normal running order of liturgical spaces in order to throw a party, because that's the way we are.

Our much celebrated and much maligned Anglican comprehensiveness is born, not of weakness or uncertainty, but out of a desire to pack everyone in if we possibly can—the more the merrier. We wish to see no one turned away, and if people wish to slip away later without saying thank you, then that's their own affair. Of course this can lead us into becoming at times over-generous and indulgent, rather than loving and kind, but that's a price we are willing to pay.

Nevertheless, despite all our well-intentioned bungling, we cling to the hope that we are on the right trail. We have a hunch that this welcome-mat way of carrying on has something to do with Jesus' vision for the Kingdom. By learning these good habits, we hope not to be *too* surprised at the number of "untouchables" who we shall find got there ahead of us.

Doing things properly

I might have called this section "tradition," had not the word been so tarnished by those who claim it to describe putting their heads in the sand in the desperate hope that when they pull them out again the earth will be found to be flat after all. Perhaps "doing things properly" says it better. Anglicans like things done well, and often this means done as they've always been done; we are an instinctively conservative lot on the whole. This is a pain for anyone called to a little moving and shaking, but at the same time has to be recognized as a major ingredient of the glue that has held us together all these centuries.

A look at the concept of ministry within the Church will immediately reveal us in our true colors. If anyone should ever doubt which side of the Reformation bed we jumped out of to begin our new life of independence from Rome, we have only to consider our deeply held conviction that important jobs can only be carried out by people with bits of white plastic round their necks, and very important jobs only by people in purple shirts. In proper parlance, this simply means we have a very high regard for episcopacy.

The downside of this reverence for episcopally ordained ministry is that we have tended to clericalize anything that moves "up front." Anyone who moves out of their seat to play a part in worship is likely to be kidnapped, taken to the sacristy, and trussed up in an alb (always too short and tied around the middle like a sack of potatoes), or (if they sing) in a cassock and surplice, in order to make the point that ministry is the prerogative of a crypto-sacerdotal caste.

All this is changing as we rediscover the vision of the first Christian communities with their dynamic concept of ministry as a whole host of gifts brought to the assembly of the faithful by every single member, to be celebrated and shared under the presidency of the overseer who was both authorized from above and affirmed from below.

Our innate conservatism has, however, played an important role in preserving us over the centuries from the worst excesses of the iconoclast so that we hold together treasures both old and new. We are a bit slower on the uptake than churches with a strong, centralized structure or not much structure at all. We allow people to hedge their bets over the simplest step forward (such as the current liturgical revision), but we somehow get there in the end, and are all the more certain of our choices for having taken our time to decide.

Exploration

Our conservatism is only half the story (and fortunately not quite a full fifty percent), for Anglicans, despite all the pressures to go on doing things they've always done, also have a proud record of breaking new ground. T. S. Eliot's affirmation that "we shall not cease from exploration" is a good maxim for all Anglicans.[1] Our size, strength, depth, variety and occasional bloody-mindedness are enough to guarantee that we are always setting out on new journeys, for above all we are a people of *hope*. We believe travel in itself to be a godly thing, and give little consideration to whether or not we have arrived.[2] Anglicans are able therefore to live with provisionality; it's not a disgrace to say "I don't know" or "I'm a bit of an agnostic on that one," and we're fond of quoting Father Raymond Raynes, who, when asked by an earnest evangelist, "Are you saved?" replied, "I'm damned if I know."[3] More than being quick-witted, this was good Anglican theology.

Whether it's pushing back the frontiers of theological debate, thinking the unthinkable about who Jesus really was, ordaining women to the priesthood and episcopate, authorizing the village "headman" to preside at the Eucharist, planting new churches in pubs on housing estates, pioneering designer-worship for our alienated young people, rethinking what church means in a post-Christian culture—in all these areas Anglicans have been in the forefront of change. Newman may have been misguided when he

26

left home, but he was dead right when he said, "To grow is to change, and to become perfect is to have changed often."

Because we are free to think for ourselves, because we are confident enough to take risks, because we are unencumbered with a weighty magisterium, and yet also because we feel secure in the sacred tradition that is ours, we are able to sally forth into the unknown to seize hold of truth. Bishop John Robinson of Woolwich wrote that we need never be afraid of the truth, wherever it leads us, and in so saying he distilled the essence of Anglicanism.[4] We are people on the move, emerging from a safe position to take hold of life with quiet, unassuming confidence.

Bishop David Jenkins put it superbly when he said, "Once a valid question has been raised, there is no going back on it, if you believe in God. There is only going forward from it. . . . Growth in the knowledge of God, as all the saints have known, is growth into the unknown."[5] As Anglicans we learn to be people on the move, emerging from safe positions to take hold of truth and of life with quiet, unassuming confidence. This is indeed the "hope God has set before us."

5 From Chains to CD Rom

The Anglican Approach to Scripture

If we make a start with the Bible, the typical characteristics of the Anglican approach will soon come into play, for we approach Scripture in the same way that we approach many other things in the Christian life—with reverence and with affection, but without working ourselves up into a lather about it.

There's an old story that does the rounds about a Baptist lady from the Deep South who, concerned about an Episcopalian friend's lack of biblical knowledge, presented her with a copy of the holy book. Her Episcopalian friend was touched and delighted, and went away to delve into its pages. A few days later she reported back excitedly that it was indeed a lovely book and had "so many nice quotes from the Prayer Book."

The Bible—really a library of books rather than a book—consists of twenty-seven early documents preserved from the first Christian communities (the New Testament), preceded by thirty-nine books making up the Hebrew Scriptures (the Old Testament), the latter, of course, familiar to Jesus himself as sacred texts. The selection of books to be kept in this particular library was the responsibility of the religious authorities of the time. The Church took until the late fourth century to agree which books were in and which were out, while leaders of the Jewish community did a similar job on the Hebrew Scriptures, finally discarding the additional books approved by Greek-speaking Jews (you will find these in some Bibles listed under the heading the Apocrypha in a kind of no-man's-land between Old and New Testaments). So the revelation of God in Scripture is process as well as event.

The story of how the Bible ended up in the size and shape it is now is one very good reason why Anglicans come to value common sense as one of the highest virtues of the spiritual life. We have learnt over the centuries to apply bucketfuls of salt to many of the things we've been told by religious fanatics, with the result that while it's fair to say we Anglicans honor Scripture, reverence it and delight in it, we fall short of worshiping it.

In fact we treat it with caution, because, like dynamite, it can blow up in our faces. Just when we're beginning to enjoy ourselves with the Bible, getting to the point of scriptural agility, tossing texts about like a juggler, we recall the warning of Jesus against people who love texts and have their noses buried in a holy book: "You search the scriptures because you think that in them you have eternal life . . . yet you refuse to come to me to have life" (John 5:39–40). Of course, Jesus was referring here to the Jewish scriptures he knew and revered from boyhood, but nevertheless the warning stands. As Anglicans see it, Christians are a people richly blessed with a priceless collection of Holy Scriptures, but they are people *with* a book, not *of* a book. Anglicans are uneasy with the notion of scriptural inerrancy, for there is more to our experience of God than even the Scriptures can encapsulate and convey. God always evades our best efforts to contain him, and the thought that we could ever box God in between the covers of a book is to be resisted. Our God is bigger than that.

But the Bible is indeed God's "Holy Word." It is the message of God to his people, gathered and set down by the human agency of those who over thousands of years have waited on the Lord in fear and trembling and excitement. Through their faithfulness, the individual believer now has in the Scriptures immediate and direct access to the mysteries of God.

As always, however, it is the middleman who gets in the way and takes too much of a cut. No one is capable of serving as a faultless audio-typist to God. Every human agent who through the centuries has played a part in setting down what we now call Holy Scripture, has had an angle, an agenda, a prejudice, or simply a failing of some kind, which has to some extent muddied the clear waters of the original revelation.

When we first sit down to read the Bible, perhaps with the fresh enthusiasm of a new believer, we may begin by imagining that God somehow arranged for his words to be miraculously transferred to the inscribed papyrus or printed page, as if by some celestial fax machine. The reality is more like a message being shouted across a busy road at the rush hour; traffic noise gets in the way and every now and then we miss a vital word. Those of us gathered on this side of the road look to each other hopefully and do our best to agree on the gist of what was being communicated, but when we compare notes we find our individual versions don't exactly coincide.

So alongside the glory and the beauty and the drama of Holy Scripture, we have too the muddle and the mistakes that typify any joint enterprise between God and humankind.

When it comes to the Bible, a number of things help Anglicans keep our feet on the ground. First, there are the limitations imposed by the Bible's multiple authorship and huge time-span of composition, rendering it virtually impossible ever to discern a single unified biblical view. Even on issues that at first glance seem self-evident, such as the sanctity of human life, it would take just a moment for an opponent to come up with a host of scriptural references to support a contrary view. History shows that Scripture can be used to support just about anything at all, from apartheid to slavery. Anglicans are therefore understandably and instinctively suspicious of those who confidently assert, "The Bible tells me so." What the speaker really means is: "My selection of certain books or texts in the Bible, influenced by my own pre-determined agenda, tells me so." We might just as well say, "The Religion section at my local library tells me so."

Again, Bishop David Jenkins puts the Anglican position well: "Our God must be the God of truth, and he cannot be served by any pretences whatsoever. If, in fact, we pretend, in the face, for instance, of careful comparison of the text of the Gospel of Mark with the text of the Gospels of Luke and Matthew that it is still possible to hold that every word of the Bible is directly dictated by God, then we are cheating and so in effect blaspheming against the God who is truth."[1]

Second, there is the matter of the integrity of each of the constituent books or letters, especially in the New Testament, and their interrelation. When we examine, for example, the differences between Mark's introduction of the adult Jesus at the beginning of his account with the miraculous birth stories with which Matthew and Luke begin their accounts, what should we say is really important? What is the essential, irreducible minimum of the Christian story? Where they differ, which account should we believe?

Then there are all those tall stories impossible for us to swallow today (and I don't just mean Jonah and the whale) which, if we were to take the biblical accounts at face value, would require us to believe that the world was created in a week, not 4700 million years, or that there was an historical character called Adam from whose rib was cobbled together Woman Number 1.

In all this it is self-evident that, while the Bible remains true in ways which are beyond rational thought, nevertheless it has its limitations. Scripture is holy, but we have to wrestle with it, as Jacob wrestled with God (Gen. 32:24), if it is to yield up its secrets and share with us its holiness. Sometimes the messages of God found in Scripture hurtle themselves at us with bruising directness and efficacy, but equally often they are far from self-evident, and have to be dug out laboriously from long stretches of unrelieved monotony or from puzzling encounters which, at first reading, have no apparent relevance to our own time and place. God is in there, struggling to get out, but to allow him to speak we have to pry apart a few bars, or even open a few doors.

Many new doors and openings have been created over the last 150 years or so by critical biblical scholarship which has sought to crack the code of Scripture that for subsequent generations of believers can so often seem a secret, forgotten language. By dissecting and analyzing the language and thought-forms and hidden agendas of those servants of God who compiled the Scriptures for us, the essential message of God can be revealed as if for the first time.

This sounds like a risky enterprise, and we must be sure not to throw out babies with the bathwater, but it is a process we need to go through if we are ever to grow up. This process is particularly important in the area of Christian evangelization, where we need to squash once and for all the quaint notion that (for example) the first chapters of Genesis are a physics textbook instead of a camp-fire story from a relatively primitive society with amazingly accurate insights into the mystery of God, and into humankind's relationship with God, present and absent. Sadly, Anglicans often feel at a disadvantage with those who are able to do conjuring tricks with scriptural texts, but we need to be more bold in asserting that proof texts rarely prove anything, and to use the Scriptures so is to abuse them. The Bible is at base a love story, not a legal encyclopedia.

Although it has been German-speaking theologians who have led the way in this exploration beyond the boundaries of what was safe and acceptable, it is a journey in which Anglicans instinctively become involved, an involvement entirely in keeping with the history of an island nation which learnt early on that survival lay in exploration far away from the safe harbors of home waters. When it comes to Scripture, Anglicans are most at ease when being thoroughly open about the anomalies evident in the Bible, not trying to pretend (for example) that every letter in the New Testament with Paul's name at the top was necessarily written by him, or that every single word ascribed to Jesus in the four Gospels was necessarily spoken by him. We like to come clean, rather than claiming for ourselves or for Scripture an authority which is impossible to uphold and which would require us to weave and dive with too-clever-by-half arguments for sustaining the unsustainable. It is not the Anglican way to keep the stable door shut after the horse has bolted.

We realize that unless we are open about these things we shall risk losing those who seek Jesus but who are unwilling to leave their brains at the door. We remain fearful lest they, in discounting the unsustainable aspects of traditional teaching, dismiss the essential good news of Jesus who is the Christ.

Today, thanks to the initiative of lone prophetic voices (with the courage to speak what everyone else is thinking) and of groups of scholars such as the Jesus Seminar, there is a growing impatience with that which is unsupportable from the facts at our disposal, and a growing acceptance of a whole host of conclusions arising from painstaking scholarship which has reopened our eyes to what was really going on in the early Christian communities that put together what we now know as the New Testament. Among the most well-established examples is the recognition of the last eleven verses of Mark's Gospel as a later addition to give a tidy and happy ending to the original form of the earliest Gospel, because the second and third generations of Christians could not face up to the rawness of Mark's ending on a note of fear and disarray (16:8).

Although the search for the historical Jesus can never be an exact science, the search for the most probable corpus of his authentic sayings is fruitful and, dare we say, fun. The question "Who really was Jesus?" is the greatest mystery thriller of all time, but to become enthralled by it, we must approach it like a good detective; with our minds open and our preconceptions kept firmly in their place.

Likewise the Fourth Gospel, attributed to John, is now recognized as a much later account than the other three (synoptic) Gospels, and one which bears the marks of the particular situation in which it was produced: the fate of Jewish Christians expelled from their synagogues in what might today be comparable to an extremely messy divorce. This explains the bitterness of the term *the Jews*, used by the author to refer to his former co-religionists, and the way in which Jesus is depicted asserting claims about himself in a manner entirely foreign to the synoptic gospels.

When we turn to the writings of Paul, it is now generally accepted that of the thirteen letters attributed to Paul, only seven can be recognized without dispute as authentic (Romans, 1 and 2 Corinthians, Galatians, Philippians, 1 Thessalonians and

Philemon). If we take a closer look at the two letters addressed to the Thessalonians, we find that although both bear Paul's name, only the first is accepted without question as his creation. The similarities between the two letters in structure and in vocabulary may point not to a common authorship (as was originally thought), nor to a wish by the author of 2 Thessalonians to comment on Paul's first edition, but perhaps even to an attempt to *replace* Paul's work.[2]

Throughout the New Testament we can detect signs of that very human tendency to dot *i*'s and cross *t*'s, reading back into earlier events later developments in thought and claiming apostolic authority for documents compiled later by those understandably concerned for the unity and stability of a volatile Christian community rent by theological disputes and struggles for ecclesiastical power. An example of this tendency is the second letter attributed to Peter. When examined carefully it is seen to contain more than enough evidence to secure a safe conviction of its author on a charge of what we would today call forgery, but what was then seen as fully justified expediency for the common good.[3]

We are concerned here not with the arguments for preferring one text as opposed to another, but with the theological battle for the mind of the newly emergent Christian Church, and for the mind of the thinking enquirer today. Anglicans believe that by understanding our Scriptures better, we can open the door onto the living Church of the first two centuries, warts and all, when nothing was as clear-cut (not even the preeminent position of Paul) as the triumphant Church of later centuries would have us believe, and when everything was up for grabs, even the deepest question of who Jesus really was.

Scripture nevertheless has a preeminent place as the body of sacred writings "containing all things necessary to salvation." For Anglicans it is placed alongside the three other articles of faith–creed, sacraments and episcopacy–enshrined for us in the Lambeth Quadrilateral (we shall come back to this in the next chapter, on doctrine). Thus Scripture is seen as one of four basic foundation stones underpinning the full and authentic Christian life, but is first among equals, being the primary source of authority in the determination of faith necessary to salvation. Its interrelatedness to the other foundations of Christian life nevertheless remains undeniable.

Drive through the urban fringe of any downtown area in America and you will see for yourself the consequences of Scripture understood in isolation. On every street corner there is a "Mom and Pop" church (Pastor and Founder: Bishop so-and-so), each with a name (for example, the True Church of God's Eternal Word) proclaiming exclusive rights to the one and only correct interpretation of Scripture, having splintered from the church along the street equally sure it enjoys a monopoly when it comes to proclaiming the "true" biblical faith. As the sole criterion for authentic Christian life, the Bible just doesn't work. To assert otherwise is to make no allowance for the wiles and weakness of human nature, which has a proven inability to approach the word on the page without bias or imbalance. It should come as no surprise that Scripture provides a shaky foundation, for unless it is complemented by tradition and reason, it remains a one-legged stool.

Our medieval forebears who chained up their Bibles were acknowledging that Scripture is a powerful force which can be used or abused, just like any of God's other gifts.[4] Today we reflect contemporary society in preferring completely open access in every conceivable way and with the help of every kind of technological gadgetry.

Anglicans have always been in the forefront of the work of translating the Bible afresh into the language of today. This task was begun by Wycliffe as early as the fourteenth century, and was taken up courageously by Tyndale (who came to a grisly end for his trouble) and Coverdale, and continues to this day with a wide range of modern translations now available to bring alive the timeless Word of God.[5] The role of the community of faith as guardians of Scripture is therefore recognized as an unavoidable part of the process if the message of God is to be reinterpreted for each new generation of believers. This role was recognized in Scripture itself in the Ethiopian eunuch's reply to Philip, on being asked whether he understood the prophecy of Isaiah that he was reading: "How can I, unless someone guides me?" (Acts 8:31). At the same time we operate as a community under the authority of Scripture. The relationship is mutual; the Church needs the Bible, and the Bible needs the Church.

The fact that our history has witnessed all these stages of biblical understanding gives us Anglicans both a sense of awe and wonder at the voice of God communicated by Holy Scripture, the word that is "living and active, sharper than any two-edged sword, piercing until it divides soul from spirit" (Heb. 4:12), and at the same time a sense of joyous excitement as we unpack this priceless gift, knowing that with the unwrapping of each layer we draw closer to the mystery of God himself who is too big and too magnificent ever to be contained between the covers of a single book.

6 Dogmas and Dugouts
The Anglican Approach to Doctrine

When it comes to the formulation of right belief, Anglicans tend not to make waves. We are conscious of being but one shard of the broken vessel which is the Church, and the junior partner in the tripartite family of churches (the Orthodox and the Roman Catholics being the other two) that claim an apostolic succession from the earliest Christian times down to the present day.

This chapter on Anglican doctrine ought to be the shortest in the book for the simple reason that Anglicanism has no doctrines of its own, being content with those inherited from the undivided Church.[1] These basic Christian doctrines are the building blocks of Christianity as a world religion, and concern chiefly the nature of God revealed as Father through Scripture and through history, the person and work of Jesus, the Christ of God, and the activity of the Holy Spirit. The Church's preoccupation with the relationship between these three manifestations of the personal God in history—these three "persons" of the Holy Trinity—sometimes suggests to others that we are unreliable monotheists. It is absolutely essential, however, that we get one thing straight from the start;

that for us as for all Christians there is only *one* God—Yahweh, Allah—and we therefore take our rightful place alongside all the other spiritual sons and daughters of Abraham in the Jewish and Islamic traditions.[2]

In matters of doctrine Anglicans attach the greatest importance to operating in accordance with what the Church believed and practiced before it was torn apart in the Great Schism of 1054, when Rome and Constantinople finally parted company. We are not interested in developing doctrines of our own, only in being faithful to the common mind of the Church of the first millennium. We strive to reproduce nothing less than that, and certainly nothing more. In determining what the early Church believed and practiced, we are therefore guided chiefly by the record of Scripture and by the documents of the General Councils of the undivided Church—the occasional formal gatherings of bishops from the four corners of the known world to deliberate on matters of doctrine and to settle disputed theological questions.

Even here, however, we try to approach these "glory days" of the early Church realistically, and with the wry thought that nothing ever really changes. We are well aware that those Councils were often summoned at the behest of an emperor who fancied his chance as an amateur theologian (Henry VIII was nothing new), or were contrived to occur when all the bishops of the opposing view happened to find themselves at the other end of the Empire with no time to pack a suitcase. Condemnations in absentia were an especially favorite trick in hurrying along theological debate at the expense of those unable to speak for themselves.[3]

An example of a document emanating from a General Council which became a primary source of authority in doctrinal matters is the profession of faith we now know as the Nicene Creed. This important summary of the basic Christian doctrines was approved by the Council of Chalcedon in 451, but possibly dates back to the Council of Constantinople in 381. This creed has been recited at eucharistic worship in both East and West ever since, and is a good example of a document which is all the more significant for having been forged in the furnace of theological controversy, every sentence and phrase representing a hard-won victory for what came to be recognized as mainstream Christian belief.

The nearest thing we have to a "foundation document" is the Lambeth Quadrilateral (or more accurately the Chicago-Lambeth Quadrilateral), which began life at the 1886 General Convention of the Episcopal Church, held in Chicago. This crossed the Atlantic two years later to be formally adopted by all the Anglican bishops meeting at Lambeth. These four Articles of Faith were seen as a good recapitulation of the essential foundations on which Anglicans stood and which helped define their unique place in the Christian family as a church both Catholic and Reformed. The four Articles, enshrining the inherent balance characteristic of Anglicanism, have proved themselves to be an invaluable benchmark in determining doctrinal questions from an Anglican point of view. They are:

- Holy Scripture as "the rule and ultimate standard of faith"
- the Apostles' and the Nicene Creeds as "sufficient statement of the Christian Faith"
- the two sacraments of Baptism and the Eucharist
- the historic episcopate.

Although divided from the Orthodox Churches by more miles and by a more distinctly different culture than is the case with Rome, it is interesting to note that when we come to doctrinal *instincts*, we find ourselves more at home with the Church of the East (centered originally on Constantinople, modern-day Istanbul) than with the Church of the West (centered on Rome).

When faced with an impenetrable mystery of God, the instinct of the East is to bow down and worship; the instinct of the West is to reach for a microscope and attempt to analyze what is going on. To take the Eucharist as one example, all three traditions hold firmly to the doctrine of the Real Presence of Christ—that in the Church's breaking of bread we can encounter Jesus as objective reality not dependent on subjective feeling—but only Rome seeks to *explain* it. The doctrine of transubstantiation, perfected by Thomas Aquinas in the thirteenth century, represents the Western tendency to take the petals off the flower in order to understand its beauty. In contrast, the Orthodox are content to approach the Eucharist as an unfathomable mystery of God which it is futile to try to explain further. This instinct is echoed in the Anglican approach to this central act of Christian worship, which Elizabeth I summed up better than anyone before or since:

> 'Twas God the word that spake it,
> He took the bread and brake it;
> And what the word did make it;
> That I believe and take it.[4]

The 1662 Book of Common Prayer, although long past its sell-by date as a source of liturgical practice for today, remains significant because it has for so long enshrined Anglican doctrinal instincts and continues to do so, now supplemented in England by *Common Worship 2000*. The old adage *lex orandi, lex credendi* (what we pray, we believe) accurately affirms that our belief is shaped by our prayer and our practice when we meet together in the assembly of the faithful.

For this reason, the work of the Liturgical Commission of the Church of England today has a significance far beyond the composition of prayers and the shaping of services. Its recent publications such as *The Promise of His Glory* (1991) show how modern liturgy can be creative, stimulating and beautiful, and at the same time formative in contemporary doctrinal understanding. Contemporary liturgy is proving itself, most notably in England and New Zealand, less so in the United States, a most effective means, for all but the most rabid reactionary, of forming worshiping communities where praying and believing are in fruitful conversation.

The deeply held conviction that we should not proceed in doctrinal matters beyond the bounds set by Holy Scripture means that Anglicanism shrinks instinctively from new dogmatic definitions which have no basis in Scripture and little or no corroboration from the Church of the first Christian centuries.

For Anglicans, Scripture has a preeminent place as the body of sacred writings "containing all things necessary to salvation," and it is Scripture that is the overriding formative influence when it comes to matters of Christian doctrine. For this reason

Canterbury parts company with Rome when it comes to the fundamental question of the definition of essential Christian beliefs. While the Roman Catholic Church feels justified in adding to the original corpus of Christian doctrines other doctrines not found in Scripture but developed by the Church over the centuries,[5] such a move into areas of belief devoid of clear scriptural warranty remains alien to the Anglican character. While it is permissible for individual Anglicans to hold such views as personal pious opinions, the adoption of such dogmas as life-and-death doctrinal matters would appear both unnecessary and harmful. Furthermore, the Anglican view would be that no single fragment of the divided Church (albeit the largest fragment) has the authority to go its own way in matters of doctrine.[6]

At the same time, Anglicanism does not shrink from radical change whenever it receives a heavy hint from the Holy Spirit, for it has always accepted that in doctrinal matters a process of evolution is going on as the Church unpacks the glorious gifts of God, peeling away the wrapping paper of the previous centuries.

This evolutionary process was very much in evidence in the development of Cranmer's eucharistic theology, for example, and in our own day can be seen in the decision to push ahead with the admission of women to the ordained priesthood in advance of the Roman and Orthodox Communions. Following the example set by other provinces and diocese of the Anglican Communion (Hong Kong 1971, Canada 1976, and the USA 1977), the Church of England ordained its first women priests in 1994, and women have now been admitted to the episcopate in Canada, New Zealand, and the United States. Although conservatives view this development with alarm, wary of such an abrupt departure from Catholic tradition, it is generally agreed that Catholic doctrine remains unimpaired. If the progressives (both Roman and Anglican) are to be believed, then it is quite inevitable that in due course the ordination of women to the presbyterate will become possible throughout the whole of the Catholic Church. Protestations of "impossibility" are not to be taken too seriously; in the seventeenth century the Roman Church said as much about the findings of Copernicus and Galileo.

With a bit of luck the Anglican Communion may therefore end up looking prophetic. Of course, being us, we didn't *mean* to be prophetic, we just did it, some of us for all the wrong reasons, and some of us with great reluctance. It would be nice however if, when the history books come to be written, Anglicans came up smelling of roses, just for once.

The fact that the Church of England sets such great store by the doctrine of the undivided Church does not mean that doctrinal questions in today's Church are a dead duck. In England, we have a Doctrine Commission to keep us on track, advising the bishops on doctrinal questions of current concern, and producing reports on thorny issues. Much of its work involves the translation of the theological language and thought-forms of the first centuries into concepts that stand a chance of being understood in today's culture.[7]

More important than the work of any commission, however, is the very air we Anglicans breathe. Anglicanism's most precious possession, and perhaps its most distinctive mark, is its creation of a church environment in which enquiry and exploration can thrive.[8] Being relatively decentralized, we have no awesome machinery for suppressing theological speculation or hounding the theologian who lives on the edge. We are free. We seek, not conformity to intellectual straitjackets imposed by yesterday's Church, but the truth.[9]

In his *Pursuit of the Ideal*, the late Isaiah Berlin wrote, "those who rest on comfortable beds of dogma are victims of forms of self-induced myopia, blinkers that may make for contentment, but not for understanding of what it is to be human." He was writing there of the futility of the human search for any perfect solution, any complete answer, but in so doing unwittingly gave expression to a very Anglican approach to dogmatic theology.

"What are certainties for others, for you are merely hints, indications, outlines." The great spiritual director Abbé Huvelin of St. Augustin, Paris, wrote these words to Baron Von Hugel at the turn of the nineteenth century, but he might even more appropriately have been addressing his kindred spirits in the Anglican Communion. He went on: "The living truth flees definitions in every direction. . . . The Scholastics do not understand that life, all life, escapes analysis. What they dissect is the dead body. . . . Pass them by, with a gentle, very gentle, smile; pass them by."[10] Our sentiments entirely.

This is no new phenomenon. The great fifth-century battle between the rigid, unyielding dogmatism of Augustine and the experiential, commonsense approach of Pelagius resulted in a predictable victory for Goliath, and the Church has had to try ever since to live with Augustine's "savage affirmation of predestination"[11] and his preoccupation with the worthlessness of humankind. The Pelagian concept of human partnership with God and the vital role of free choice have been tut-tutted against ever since. Not just because we tend to back the underdog, or because Pelagius was British through and through, but also because we have a deep distrust of massive, water-tight systems which allow no room for individual maneuver, we Anglicans tend to remain uneasy about Pelagius's confinement in the sin-bin while Augustine's obsessions continue to ricochet around the Church unchallenged.

To dig itself deep into defensive dogmatic dugouts is not therefore the Anglican way. It prefers a more relaxed approach. This can be difficult to live with at times, but occasional pain and frustration are a price worth paying for the glorious privilege of a life in a sacred community where fear and intimidation are unknown concepts. Because of this freedom we enjoy a real sense both of receiving doctrine from the past, and of participating together in the ceaseless process of reinterpreting and renewing it for the future.

7 Us and Me
The Anglican Approach to the Church

Subway trains in any big city are sometimes potentially dangerous places, but I am not talking here of the threat of physical harm, but of the conversations we may overhear that could seriously damage our spiritual health.

One conversation I once overheard on the London Tube involved a middle-aged man stringing off to his companion a list of all the churches he had belonged to over the last thirty years in different parts of the world—an Anglican one here, a Baptist there, a Pentecostal over here. He had in fact reverted to Anglicanism in the end, but I doubt that he was much of a catch. He was a product of our times, of the consumerist attitude that proclaims the gospel of picking and choosing to suit our own needs, soft-peddling brand loyalty.

Significantly, experience of Roman Catholicism was missing from his list, indicating an evangelical allegiance, and this highlights for us the spectrum of widely differing attitudes to the Church. We might call this the spectrum of ecclesiology, at one end of which is "me" and at the other is "us." Our friend on the train would have been at the far left, the "me" end of the spectrum, concerned chiefly with the individual's relationship with

47

God, whereas the practicing Roman Catholic or Orthodox would be at the far right, the "us" end of the spectrum, concerned chiefly with the incorporation of the individual into the corporate life of the Body of Christ.

It won't come as a big surprise to know that Anglicanism maintains a steady middle position in this spectrum, holding the balance between the individual and the corporate aspects of life in the Church. The Church can be built only from living stones, from individual men and women who know their need of God, with whom they have entered a personal relationship. That being said, the Church is a great deal more than the sum of its individual members, and when energized by the Spirit, it takes on a life of its own. The living Church is truly a mystery of God, and becomes, as it were, a person in its own right, with its own demands on our time and on our loyalty.

Once again, as with Scripture, we see in the Anglican approach to the Church that characteristic combination of reverence and affection tempered by common sense and a refusal to take too seriously the assertions of the partisan. It doesn't escape our attention that those Christian churches most convinced of the divine authority of their magisterium are precisely the churches most likely to exalt man-made rules into God-given commandments. Such observations confirm us in our preference for a more relaxed approach, a less exalted notion of our own importance in the economy of God.

The word *church* has been much abused over the centuries. Originally meaning the assembly of the faithful, it has been gradually debased so as to come to mean the building in which the assembly meets. It is the latter definition that takes preference in the dictionaries and in common use. We talk glibly of *going to church* when all the time the wonder of God's design is that we are called to *be* church. Once we recall the dynamic rather than the static meaning of the word, we begin to glimpse the many-layered meanings of *church* for us today.

Most commonly, *church* is the symbol of our allegiance, the word used to describe the local Christian community, where we encounter God and which is the focus of our activity and endeavors as Christians. Interestingly, the application of this word continually widens, and is now most frequently used for the regular assembly of believers, irrespective of their ecclesiology or background.[1]

Church in the localized sense means our Nazareth: the one-horse town, full of misfits, clowns and the walking wounded, of which we are part. Here God has chosen to place us so that we can give him glory and help to establish his Kingdom. Such particular and localized allegiance is an inescapable part of our growing up into God. Without our thirty years in Nazareth we shall never be equipped to do our three years' active service.

This is why it is so important for us to become part of a church and to stick with it. Not because our church is better than yours, but simply because every single local church, big or small, good, bad or indifferent, is able to be for us God's hot-house, where we, his prize plants, can be nurtured and brought to maturity. Such nurture is, however, not always a case of basking in warm sunshine; a hot-house is a place of forcing growth when our natural inclination is to stagnate. The local church is a place where we have the corners knocked off us, and come face to face with the variable and unreliable quality of the raw material (you and me) at God's disposal. It can be an exhausting and bruising process, but then so is winning the Super Bowl or scaling Everest. Because Anglican communities of faith tend to be small to medium in size, you may feel very exposed, soon noticed if you are present, but immediately missed if you're not. You will be entering a real community, not conducive to anonymity, and the writing is on the wall for those who, in their anxiety to avoid participation, will lurk behind pillars, sit in the back row, or confine themselves to eight o'clock Communion.

In England, the local church will serve a parish, a chunk of territory defined precisely in geographical terms, which serves to give its members an added dimension to the Nazareth experience. It is not only your fellow-worshipers to whom you are connected, but also the whole population of men, women and children—irrespective of religious affiliation—who live within the parish boundaries.

This is mistakenly thought to have something to do with the Church of England's position "by Law Established," but this is not so. It arises from a historic sense of apostolic commission, a conviction clouded and undermined, rather than enhanced, by the illusory advantages of Established status. This has been true from Constantine onward, but we are just a little slow on the uptake.

The church with a small *c*, the "local branch," is symbolized for Episcopalians and for Canadian Anglicans, too, by a dinky building of imitation gothic, with pointed windows of stained glass and dark interiors, crowded with black furniture, rails and screens and much red carpet. Somewhere along the line the Anglican community in North America decided to major in quaintness, and for many Episcopalians the gothic fantasy seems to define what they are. Even "modern" church buildings of the last fifty years perpetuate the long tunnel approach to liturgical space, and it isn't long before the architect's vision of a light-filled interior is destroyed by the benefactors who line up to insert stained glass in every opening.

So although Anglicans in North America are not weighted down with buildings of great antiquity, we might as well be so, such is our subservience to this one particular physical expression of our identity, without which we get disoriented or even panic stricken. This has serious repercussions for our sense of mission, which is seen not so much as sharing good news with all and sundry as it is making connections with our kind of people. Charles Fulton, Director of Congregational Development for the Episcopal Church, has described evangelism for Episcopalians as "getting dressed up and waiting for people to call," and I myself have heard arguments for not beginning a new mission church in an expanding suburban area based on the criterion that "there aren't many Episcopalians there." Precisely so! That's exactly why we *need* a mission there. But if our true agenda is to provide little gothic boxes for people who like that kind of thing, then we have nothing to say to the world. Our apostolic commission to proclaim good news to the ends of the earth has been replaced by a limited program of "expanded facilities for existing customers."

Just to make it really interesting, the parish church in England is "home," in a quite different way, to all the people who stay away from it. Local inhabitants who claim even the vaguest Christian label, irrespective of tradition, will all have a proprietary interest in this building which they consider in some mysterious way to be *theirs*; a place to have recourse to as the need arises, irrespective of Christian belief and practice. Here parish churches are like branch railway lines; too few use them until closure or curtailment of services is threatened. Thereupon the whole community is awash with posters and car-stickers, and you can't emerge from your front door without falling over a woman with a clip-board asking you to sign a petition. This is the church: the local corner shop, God's post office on your street.

Under the direction of its parish priest, every parish church has an apostolic commission to share the good news of Jesus Christ with the people God has put in their patch. This is a great privilege, which other Christian traditions in England would give their right arm for in terms of evangelistic opportunity.

As things stand, you've chosen a good moment to think of enlisting, as you've arrived just in time to take part in the revolution. In the bad old days (up to today), the local church meant the parish priest (*vicar* is a terrible word nowadays, redolent of limp wrists and cucumber sandwiches) supported to a larger or lesser extent by a small band of helpers. The cataclysmic changes in the culture around us—which evidence spiritual hunger coupled with a distaste for the church's regular menu—demand a radical rethinking of what *church* means now. This will involve the mobilization of the whole community of faith, with the ordained leader accepting a rewritten job description as trainer and enabler rather than a one-man worship and mission team. The priest's primary role is to be a holy man or woman of God, recalling us to our full potential—corporately as the holy community of faith, and individually as human beings for whom humanity is redefined by Jesus. The priest conducts the orchestra, and does so most effectively when not attempting to play every instrument.[2]

Anglicans are not Congregationalists, however, despite the best attempts of some Episcopalians to make us so (if there is an Achilles' heel to the Episcopal Church it is not biblical relativism but innate congregationalism). Although life in the local church is make-or-break time for every Anglican, the place where we must pound the beat before going on to more exciting things, we are conscious of belonging to the wider Church, at diocesan and national levels.

The diocese is the area of the Church's life under the authority of a diocesan bishop. In the diocese each parish is reminded that it is merely an individual in a bigger community, and diocesan events are occasions when we celebrate this larger dimension to our Christian lives, and whoop it up a bit. Ordinations and confirmations are examples of significant events centralized at diocesan level, and presided over by our bishop (or "father in God") as an essential reminder that no parish is an island. The cathedral (so called because it houses the chair, or *cathedra*, of the bishop) is the symbolic base camp of diocesan life, our mother church, and a big cathedral event has a real sense of occasion about it for us backwoodsmen.

The cathedral is a dominant player in the team-building of diocesan life, for it is a "flagship of the Spirit."[3] Those few remaining dioceses in the United States that persist in the bizarre notion of a cathedral-less diocese (perhaps no one told them the Revolution was over?) are gradually falling into line as the penny drops. Ironically it is the Episcopal Church that needs cathedrals most, for they serve to remind us of the greater good, the larger commonwealth, in the face of the rampant congregationalism endemic to that part of our Communion.

The perception and understanding of the Church at national level will vary from person to person and from country to country. Some will see it as a religious body that will be there for us when we as a nation no longer know what to do or to say. At the funeral of Diana, Princess of Wales, in 1997, it was as if Westminster Abbey became home for all of us—whatever our creed, color or nationality, and whether we were packed inside it, or sitting on the grass in Hyde Park, or tuning in on a TV set on the other side of the planet.[4] Likewise in 2001 after 9/11, it was to the National Cathedral in Washington, DC (actually the cathedral of the *Episcopal* Bishop of Washington) that the American nation flocked, the president at their head.

Others will see the Church in administrative terms, as a legislative body (in the U.S. the General Convention centered on 815 Second Avenue in New York City; in England the General

Synod centered on Church House, Westminster); or as the organization that produces an archbishop to appear on the news when the nation's nerve needs steadying; or the bureaucracy that keeps the show on the road and sends out the salary checks every month (hey guys, you still have some pension funds left, don't you?).

In England, Anglicans find themselves in the Established Church, the only church of the Anglican Communion so fettered. The Church of England is part of the fabric of society, with legal safeguards protecting its public role and allowing the State a voice in the ordering of the Church's affairs. Although establishment confers little more than seats for senior diocesan bishops in the upper house of parliament, and a prominent role in ceremonial occasions, it is seen by the more optimistic among us as providing invaluable opportunities for a quiet unobtrusive influence for good. Others of our number see it instead as an embarrassing anachronism tending to emasculate the Church in the exercise of its spiritual and apostolic commission.

Perhaps the most depressing aspect of this debate is that there is hardly any debate at all; the status quo seems to be accepted with surprising passivity, and any talk of bringing the arrangement to an end centers on the secularization of government rather than the coming-of-age of the Church.

Certainly the English can be excused for looking enviously at those parts of the Anglican Communion such as the Episcopal Church in the United States, where the proscription of religion in government and education seems to have invigorated the life of the local church in a way no longer conceivable in England or northern Europe generally. Perhaps, after all, the English backed the wrong horse.

Just to balance the books, however, the Episcopal Church also faces many problems so endemic to its structures that it would probably take a personal appearance by the Archangel Gabriel to achieve any change in canon law. The problem is simply the imbalance of power within the Church; the basic unit being the local congregation rather than the diocese. This reduces the role of diocesan bishop to that of amiable cheerleader, and of parish priest to that of hired servant of the vestry. This imbalance between the branches and the tree manifests itself also in unseemly disputes over property whenever a local church deludes itself into thinking that it has, over against the wickedness of the high priest, discovered all for itself the Holy Grail of ecclesial purity. Because congregationalism is endemic in the system, the church concerned may well feel it has the right to take to itself that which is part of a greater whole. Disdain for episcopal authority is also a deeply Protestant instinct, yet so strangely prevalent among those who call themselves Catholic.

These problems can all be laid at the door of the Church of England, of course, which in the seventeenth and eighteenth centuries abandoned its children in the North American colonies, leaving them to their own devices and to dream up any old church polity that took their fancy. Still, we must be thankful for small mercies; given the British bungling of the Colonial era, it's a wonder that there is any Episcopal Church at all.

Be that as it may, Anglicans on both sides of the Atlantic can be said to belong to national churches which, despite increasing marginalization, retain an influence out of all proportion to their strength in numbers. In different ways they both are seen as institutions which embody a way of life, and sustain the soul of a nation. It won't do for us to be complacent, however, for though this may breed a certain affection in the minds of the populace, it's of the kind we may feel for a favorite old auntie who has lost all of her teeth and most of her mind (Archbishop Carey once said something similar, but was not thanked for his deadly accuracy). So our privileges demand of us alertness and presence of mind if we are to keep the flame of faith alive.

For most members of the Anglican Communion, the Church of England's ties to the Crown are a puzzle if not an embarrassment, but there are signs that the condition is not terminal. The Church in England now enjoys a greater degree of freedom in the ordering of its own affairs than it has since the Reformation period, and we must keep up the momentum in this respect, breaking free from the last vestiges of the State control that has proved such a heavy price to pay for the reforms of the sixteenth century. It would be good if this could be achieved with a little dignity, from positive conviction rather than by default. If the

Church of England is indeed a kept woman, as many would claim, then she needs to find the courage to walk away from the situation before being thrown out on the street.

We should not imagine that problems in the relationship between Church and State are confined to the post-Reformation period. In the twelfth century, relations between Thomas Becket, Archbishop of Canterbury, and King Henry II grew so acrimonious that Becket spent six of his eight years as primate in exile in France (although his subsequent martyrdom ensured eternal celebrity status for him and humiliation for the king). Four hundred years later, Becket's successor, Thomas Cranmer, had no concept of Church as an authority independent of the anointed king, and rushed to fill the power vacuum left by the papacy with a new definition of monarchy as a spiritual force.[5] So enraged was Henry VIII at the very thought of Becket the king-tamer that he had Becket's magnificent shrine in Canterbury Cathedral torn down and destroyed.[6]

The resilience of the Church of England under Archbishop Robert Runcie (1980–91) in recalling the nation, in the face of a hostile government, to the concept of a truly Christian society, did something to redress the balance of spiritual power. The establishment of the Church Urban Fund to reach out in compassion to those in England's inner cities, and the challenging of the notion of the Falklands conflict as a triumphal crusade, tweaked the State's tail, and did much to restore Anglican self-confidence.

Over and above the local and national definitions of what "the church" means to us is that dimension bigger than all our human definitions and earthly arrangements; the real McCoy, or as the Nicene Creed puts it, "the one, holy, catholic and apostolic Church." At this level the Church stands between heaven and earth, combining aspects which are both here-and-now and beyond time and space.

Throughout Christian history, fragments of the broken Church have from time to time attempted to claim for themselves the totality of what it means to be *the* one, holy, catholic and apostolic Church. After the Great Schism of 1054, the resultant two churches, centered on Constantinople and Rome, each maintained that it alone was the one true Church and that the other was in schism. Each church excommunicated the other, Rome becoming a breakaway sect in the eyes of Constantinople, and vice versa. Although in 1965 these mutual excommunications were quashed, the two sides are not really very much further forward, each remaining decidedly snooty about the other. This is rather reassuring for us Anglicans, about whom simply everybody is snooty most of the time.

More seriously, the posturings of the ancient churches of East and West, claiming absolute and exclusive authority and getting tangled up in the unseemly business of mutual denunciation, have provided conclusive proof that it is futile for any one part of the Church to claim to exercise the authority pertaining only to the whole. Such claims begin to look a little ridiculous once we stand back and take stock of such assertions in the context of Christian history. The Anglican view is that since the end of the undivided Church, no single fragment of it (no matter how large its membership or magnificent its structure) can make exclusive claims about authenticity. Since the Great Schism, *every* church is to some extent in schism, for we have all erred in breaking unity with one another. Faced with portentous claims from any quarter, the Anglican response is to blow a (very gentle, almost inaudible) raspberry, knowing how dangerous to the soul are pomposity and self-delusion.

One sign that we are entering healthier times is the growing use of the word *Church*, by Christians of every conceivable background (including those for whom previously it remained an empty concept), to refer to the physical reality of the whole Christian community across the world. Whenever we do so, we speak prophetically, making real the reunited Church which as yet remains beyond the reach of ecclesiastical diplomacy.

Whereas top-level talks about Church reunion continue to flounder, undermined by institutional stubbornness and fear, the most promising signs of hope are the quiet but continuous acts of loving and thoughtful rebellion at grassroots level in which individual Christians refuse to allow man-made regulations to prevent their living out the Christian life with integrity and courtesy.[7] The generous eucharistic hospitality I have nearly always encountered when traveling on the European mainland has warmed my heart, and speaks louder than all the pronouncements of the Vatican. Good manners and basic common sense may in the end save us from canon law.

Full intercommunion will never rain down upon us from above; it will bubble up from below, an unstoppable spring "welling up to eternal life." The delay in rebuilding the undivided Church has much to do with this vexed question of admission to the sacred meals celebrated by different parts of the one Church. Each of the mainstream traditions has tended to guard its table jealously, ring-fencing it with a list of necessary qualifications to restrict participation to its own membership and perhaps a few friends of the family on special occasions, but the barricades are falling.

If we stop to recall that the one most outrageous and shocking act of Jesus of Nazareth was to eat with the untouchables and riff-raff of society, then perhaps all Christian Churches will begin to see that if we are to honor this prophetic tradition of our master, then the Eucharist is the very last place to exercise discrimination and exclusion. Here at least Anglicans have played a vital role in keeping the door ajar and the table laid.

Before the mystery of the one holy, undivided community which the Church is called to be, our own needs, demands, rights or desires are seen in true perspective. As we mature in our faith, perhaps we are enabled to shuffle along a few paces, from the "me" toward the "us" end of the spectrum while remembering, of course (like the good Anglicans we are), that the Church needs lots of little *me*'s to make an *us*.

8 Bouquets and Bandages
The Anglican Approach to the Sacraments

Sacraments are funny things, and it takes an Anglican to work them out. They are the sharp points of God's love for us—the places where he actually touches us, prods us with the end of his finger—and a sense of balance is required to walk the tightrope between mere symbolism on the one hand and the confusion of sign and signified on the other. Needless to say, if there's one thing we Anglicans know about, it's balancing.

The catechism of the *Book of Common Prayer* 1979 defines sacraments as "outward and visible signs of an inward and spiritual grace"; but it is more than a sign, because a sacrament is also "a means whereby we receive the same." In other words, a sacrament is one of those signs that is so powerful that it brings about that which it signifies. If that sounds awfully like philosophical word-play, we can earth it with the parallel of sexual intercourse within marriage. Sexual union is a sign and symbol of marriage, but is far more than that, for it consummates the marriage, making it full and real.

In the sacrament of baptism, the believer undergoes a ritual washing (albeit usually in attenuated form), which is the outward and visible sign of the inward and spiritual grace of a new life lived in the Spirit which is entered via the individual's symbolic death and resurrection. This is most clearly expressed in baptism by submersion, when the candidate "dies" by drowning beneath the surface of the water, before being pulled from the water to breathe deeply of the fresh air of the community of faith, oxygenated by the Spirit of God. It is this sacrament which delineates the Christian community, the community of the baptized, the holy people of God.

In the sacrament of the Eucharist, the believer participates in the outward and visible sign of a sacred meal, consuming merely a fragment of bread and a tiny sip of wine, but entering thereby into the inward and spiritual reality of a feast which looks back to those meals of Jesus with his friends in Galilee and forward to the glorious wedding reception which is the consummation of the marriage between the Christ and his faithful people.

When we come to speak of sacraments, however, before getting carried away in devotional bliss we must do some serious penance, for in this area of its life the Christian Church must hang its head in shame. Here was one of God's very best ideas thrown back in his face. Sacraments are little presents from God, lovingly gift-wrapped in beautiful packages (refreshing water, warm bread, soothing aromatic oil) and generously provided both to encourage us at vital navigation points on our journey, and to sustain us for the regular foot-slogging of daily life. Nothing could be simpler. It seems, however, that God had not foreseen the infinite capacity of humankind to abuse the best things of creation. Nowhere is this more true than in relation to the Eucharist, of all the sacraments the one in which we encounter God most frequently.

Jesus was the wild prophet who overturned tables, both literally (in the Temple precincts) and figuratively (in his abandonment of Jewish ritual exclusivity). Jesus inaugurated the open table as the most powerful sign he could imagine of the coming Kingdom of God.[1] The open, unconditional invitation to eat at the table of Jesus was a potent symbol of the new kind of society he sought to create. The open table was also deeply subversive to religious authority, and the Christian Church (no more than the

Jewish hierarchy of Jesus' day) has never been able to cope with it. To think that for many centuries Christians murdered one another, and subjected one another to excruciating torture, all for the sake of the precise definition of what *exactly* was happening when the Church broke bread and blessed wine, is nothing less than obscene. Here was the Church hurling back at God his sign of unconditional love, setting at naught the sacrifice of the Christ, and making null and void this central and preeminent tenet of his teaching. In those dark days the Church turned the gospel on its head, and though we may recoil in horror, there are few of us completely free of those same prejudices that wrought such havoc in the past.

As good Anglicans, therefore, mindful of the blood spilt on English soil in the pursuit of theological correctness, we must approach the sacraments with a renewed reverence at the wonder of God's lavish provision, and a renewed determination to keep our grubby little hands from dirtying what is given to us pure and undefiled.

First of all we should refuse to play the numbers game. There are commonly said to be two sacraments—Baptism and the Eucharist—which Jesus indisputably set in motion himself. In addition there are five others—penance, anointing of the sick, confirmation, marriage and ordination—which those of the Catholic tradition are careful to include, albeit as "lesser" sacraments.

The truth is not likely to be that simple or that neat and tidy. In the first place, the distinction between *dominical* (those instituted by the Lord) and *lesser* sacraments seems arbitrary. Taking the Gospel passages at their face value, penance has just as good a claim as baptism (perhaps more so) to be an authentic dominical sacrament, some method by which Christians are to be reassured of God's forgiveness through the ministry of the Church, being clearly seen to form part of Jesus' intentions, at least in the Fourth Gospel (John 20:23). When we take a look at the Reformation period, we see that the Ten Articles of 1536 (two years after the break with Rome) were emphatic in asserting that auricular confession was "instituted of Christ," and the Bishops' Book of 1537 maintained the special character of these three major sacraments as distinct from the four lesser ones, which had only tradition to support them. This was the Lutheran view, and it was only later, when more Calvinist influences gained the upper hand, and the Reformers grew more jittery about priestly power, that the number of major sacraments was altered to two, politics taking precedence over biblical exegesis.

Sacramental confession therefore has always been a vital part of Anglican spiritual life, albeit in a characteristically open way—no boxes or curtains for us, thank you. It is encouraged, rather than enforced, and penitents do not confess *to* a priest, but *alongside* a priest to God, whose forgiveness needs to be made personal if we are ever to be healed of our self-inflicted wounds. Today, increasing numbers of Christians in all traditions are discovering the healing power of the Sacrament of Reconciliation, as Penance is now usually called.

When it comes to baptism, we might want to examine more closely the texts at the end of Mark's and Matthew's Gospels which exhort the Church to "get baptizing!" In the case of Mark it is almost certainly a later addition, and these postscripts may reflect not so much the priorities of Jesus himself (who showed a marked lack of interest in baptism throughout his ministry) as the early Church's concern to establish and authenticate proper procedures for initiation into the Christian community.

In the second place, we should be wary of limiting God's sacramental grace. While it is important not to devalue the currency by labeling as a sacrament every conceivable encounter with God in which the physical is used to communicate the spiritual, nevertheless in our instinctive approach to sacraments we should be shouting "not seven, but seventy times seven!" (Matt. 18:22).

In establishing its original list of seven sacraments the Church was obviously seeking to mark various key points in our life story with solemn rites and ceremonies in which the ministry of the Church could bring the blessing of God to bear on those moments when we seek to renew our covenant with God. Baptism, confirmation, ordination, and marriage are examples of "key stage" sacraments, to be experienced once only, while penance, anointing and Eucharist are designed to keep us on the road, and to be experienced over and over again. In the key stage sacraments the Church picked out just four moments for hallowing in this way, but we can imagine many more events suitable for extending this principle (for example, commissioning various forms of lay ministry, or the blessing of an individual or family before they emigrate or move to another part of the country).

A sacrament is always a communal event with a vital social dimension, celebrated by or on behalf of the community of faith. Even where the participants are limited in number (as in the sacrament of reconciliation) the community is nevertheless an unseen partner in the deal, for it is for the community's sake (as well as the penitent's) that the sacrament was given, that by reconciliation and healing, the Body of Christ might be built up and made strong. Where the Christian community prays over individuals or groups in these circumstances, laying hands upon them and anointing them with holy oil, or blessing them with water from the baptismal font, then we can safely say that a sacramental act has taken place, or even that a new sacrament has been born. Another sacrament is like another saint; we can't have too many of them.

We are in good company if we refuse to restrict God's grace in this way. The classification of the sacraments was but another typical example of the tidy little mind of the Western Church, which wanted to have everything neatly tied up into bundles, each with its own label. The classification of the sacraments wasn't even attempted for the first five hundred years (when all kinds of occasions were included such as funerals and the taking of monastic vows), and it took until 1439 for a definitive list to be finally approved.

The great thing to remember about a sacrament is this: that God always turns up, even if we are late or don't turn up at all. In other words, a sacrament conveys the *objective* reality of God's love; it is not a question of feelings, or of our subjective perception of what is going on, but of what God is actually *doing*, come what may. In this way, receiving Holy Communion (which will be a real encounter with God no matter which side of the bed we got out of that morning) is a quite different kind of encounter with God than being moved by a word of Scripture or by a particular worship song (which will depend—far too much for our own good—on our own feelings and receptiveness at any one moment).

At the Reformation, the Church of England finally came out against the teaching of people such as the Swiss reformer Zwingli, who maintained that it is only the communicant's faith that makes Christ present in the Eucharist. We are certain that the sacrament is more than a mere signpost pointing to a distant destination; it is itself a point of arrival, of encounter. Basically keeping company with Luther on this question, Anglican reformers maintained the doctrine of the Real Presence of Christ in the Eucharist (irrespective of our faith) while denouncing the need to explain that Presence further with philosophical theories such as transubstantiation.[2]

Dangers lurk on every side. When our grasp of the objective reality of a sacrament is weak and wobbly, we might easily slide into casual ways, not discerning the Lord's body (1 Cor. 11:9), even throwing to the birds the bread left over from the altar, rather than consuming it reverently as our rubrics bid us do, or reserving it in a special place (an aumbry or tabernacle) for the benefit of the sick or those at prayer. Conversely, if our emphasis on objective reality is too literal and circumscribed, we may confuse the sign for the thing signified, mistaking the sacrament of the Lord's presence for the Lord himself, becoming neurotic rather than reverent, burning the best sanctuary carpet should ever a drop be spilt on it from the chalice. That way lies idolatry.

We must also take care to safeguard the nature of sacraments as covenants between God and humankind, rather than as pieces of automatic mechanism dispensing God's grace like water from a tap. An undue emphasis on God's grace to the virtual exclusion of human response is in the end an affront to God's desire to enter into covenant with us. We grow lazy or careless of our own responsibilities in what ought to be a relationship of mutual love where God's grace meets with our willing cooperation and eager participation.

When it comes to the administration of infant baptism, especially in the English situation, where there remains considerable social pressure on the Established Church to "do the business" as and when required, Anglican practice can sometimes be reduced to the unthinking, automated movements of a robot. We too easily hide behind a theology of God's overflowing grace to justify our unwillingness to devote sufficient time and energy to working alongside enquirers, either incorporating them into the life of the Church, or developing for them appropriate rituals which will satisfy their needs without making nonsense of the Church's efforts to reinstate baptism as a meaningful sign of death-and-resurrection and initiation into lifelong commitment within the community of faith.[3]

Despite such operational difficulties, it is the genius of Anglicanism that, in rejecting a sacramental theology of, on the one hand, the automatic soft-drinks machine, and on the other, the private, sentimental journey down memory lane, it manages to hold together as perhaps no other tradition can, the complementary aspects of divine initiative and human response.

Anglicanism can reverence the sacraments without mistaking them for the reality to which they point. Anglicans retain a sense of proportion, a deep, instinctive understanding that when in solemn assembly we break bread, or pour water or anoint with oil, the Lord makes himself known to us, and we are changed.

9 Decently and in Order
The Anglican Approach to Worship

Worship is what Anglicans know about, and even our most severe critics will grudgingly admit that it's something we do well. The Anglican tradition seems to be gifted with a sixth sense where worship is concerned, and seems able to hit just the right note for the occasion,[1] whether for millions of viewers in Westminster Abbey or the National Cathedral or for two or three gathered together in an obscure country church. It knows all about dignity in worship, but about celebration too; about when to understate, and when to play the tingle factor for all it's worth.

Our worship is shaped by our history, and so tells us a lot about where we have come from. It is at worship that the Anglican communities are most clearly and immediately recognizable as belonging to the family of Catholic churches, offering the unceasing round of prayer in set forms of daily prayer (the Divine Office) and the Eucharist. These are forms of liturgical (as distinct from unstructured) prayer, in which an unchanging given framework is enlivened by variable features–readings, prayers and songs–which reflect the Church's liturgical year and respond to events of the day.

Although we've been at liturgical formation for a very long time, the Church of England put a sudden spurt on during the sixteenth century, when it had to make its mind up about whose side it was on in the religious upheaval sweeping Europe. As the attempt to reform the Roman Church from within, beginning with Martin Luther in Germany, proved unworkable, the new wine burst the old wineskin and the world was agog with new ideas about how Christians should relate to God and to each other.

As a result of this commotion, Sunday worship in the parish church came to perform the function of a TV news program today—people could tune in to what was happening on the worldwide stage, translated for their benefit into language and images they could understand. They were glued to their screens because they lived in exciting times, witnessing a sea change in the English Church—what the theologian Hans Küng would call a paradigm shift. At the same time, they felt secure: Their parish church and their parish priest gave them reassurance amid upheaval.

The hand and the pen guiding the Church of England through these cataclysmic changes were those of Thomas Cranmer, Archbishop of Canterbury 1532–56, whose desire for radical reform was matched by a gift for beautiful language. He longed to give the English people a liturgy through which they might articulate a new directness of approach to God, liberated from the abuses and superstitions of the medieval Church. In all this, Cranmer's task was made easy and impossible at the same time by Henry VIII, the king who had propelled him into the top ecclesiastical job at breakneck speed. The *Via Media* of a Catholic Church in England freed from Roman interference was really Henry's vision, and Cranmer would have achieved little without him. Henry was no mean theologian himself and believed that the Church was far too important a matter to be left to churchmen. For Cranmer, however, devising a new theological and liturgical language for the English Church with Henry breathing down his neck cannot have made for ideal working conditions.

Crucial to the new "house style" of the English Church was a new liturgy, so that those making their way to the parish church each Sunday (the vast majority of the population) would be left in no doubt that times had changed. Both the Eucharist and the

Divine Office were made accessible to the people, and more immediate and intimate in their appeal. Eucharist and Office were the weft and warp of the new fabric of worship for the English people. The English Reformers set about with a sense of excitement to peel away the accretions of medievalism to reveal once again the insights of the primitive Church. With the same enthusiasm witnessed in our own generation following Vatican II, the local church found its feet again as a participatory community of faith.

In all this Cranmer master-minded nothing less than a "turbulent liturgical revolution,"[2] an upheaval so great that in some areas of the country it was a contributory factor in civil uprising and bloodshed. It is ironic in the extreme that those, on both sides of the Atlantic, who today would attempt to justify the continued use of seventeenth-century rites should associate the name of Cranmer with the perpetuation of antiquated language in worship. Not merely spinning in his grave, he must be going into orbit. Cranmer set himself the task of re-expressing the timeless liturgy of the Church in "such language as they might understand, and have profit by hearing the same." He recognized the sterility of clinging to outmoded language (Latin then, and "Prayer Book language" today) which the faithful "have heard with their ears only," with the result that "their heart, spirit, and mind, have not been edified thereby."[3]

Cranmer enshrined these ideas in a Book of Common Prayer, the first version of which (1549), was updated (in a more Protestant direction) in 1552, and again (in a slightly more Catholic direction) in 1662, revisions which reflected the power struggles of the period in Church and State. Much midnight oil was burned attempting to capture in words and ritual the insights that were taking the Church of England into a new era, and the starting point was the sacred Christian meal, the Eucharist, at which Jesus, the Risen Lord, makes himself known to us in the breaking of the bread.

Although *Eucharist* may sound obscure and technical, it is simply the Greek for *thank you*, virtually the same word we use today on a Greek holiday when we thank the waiter at the taverna. Americans, of course, with their inspired annual celebration of Thanksgiving, need no prompting on this. The thanksgiving meal of the Eucharist is the chief act of worship for parishes Sunday by Sunday, as the whole faith community gathers to celebrate its communal life in the Risen Lord. The Anglican Communion is a eucharistic community, which is symptomatic of its essentially Catholic nature although, in company with the Orthodox, its priority is the eucharistic assembly on "the first day of the week" (Acts 20:7) and also on major festivals and saints' days. In company with the Orthodox, it does not see anything particularly primitive or desirable in an obsessive insistence on a daily celebration of the Eucharist in conditions where it ceases to become an offering of the whole community and is reduced to an act of personal piety by the few.

With the Eucharist we are again indebted to the Reformers like Cranmer who, four centuries before Vatican II, sought to make the Eucharist no longer a "muttered Mass" behind a screen, but a corporate, participatory act of worship in which all the faithful were to be made conscious of their individual value and significance within the priesthood of the whole community. Not only was the eucharistic liturgy translated into English, but the act of Communion at the heart of the Mass, which had previously been restricted to once a year at Easter, was encouraged weekly.

We can imagine the enthusiasm, in those parishes where the vision was first caught, with which the altar would have been dragged down from the east wall, turned through ninety degrees and set in the midst of the chancel where everyone could literally gather round; the altar of sacrifice, mysterious and distant, became the table of the Lord, set up in the middle of the house of the church. Just like today, we would see then the same sense of excitement among the visionaries, and the same cold water administered by those who wanted none of it, but who bided their time, hoping the next regime would put it all back again. Fortunately for us the visionaries won out in the end, though we shouldn't forget the cost–Cranmer and many others paying with their lives.

The Eucharist will be known by many different names in the Anglican tradition, as befits its consistent attempt to do justice to every aspect of this sacred meal of the Church. *Mass* is the old

English word retained as a subtitle by Cranmer in his first Prayer Book, the ancient name familiar to everyone and which gave them a reassuring sense of continuity. In the 1552 version, less conciliatory to old ways, *Mass* was dropped, and *Lord's Supper* and *Holy Communion* (the latter in slightly larger print) were allowed to stand alone, descriptions retained in the 1662 update. *Lord's Supper* never caught on, so we are left with *Holy Communion* in common parlance, a name which fails to do justice to the whole action of the eucharistic offering of praise and thanksgiving. It is greatly to be regretted that, in England, even the 2000 update, unlike new liturgies in other Anglican provinces such as the United States and Wales, perpetuates (in its primary headings) this lopsided description of the Mass. Although it did manage to insert *Eucharist* as a first subtitle, it excluded *Mass* (although in common use and primitively Anglican) while retaining *Lord's Supper* (which is neither). Ah, well, life in the Anglican Communion can't always be joy unconfined.

Today *Eucharist* is generally accepted as the best option, being a word innocent of party political overtones, recalling us to the early Church, and reminding us of the instinctive attitude of thanksgiving which should irradiate all our worship. Take time to look up *The Shape of the Liturgy* by Gregory Dix, a towering liturgical authority of the Anglican tradition, and himself a Benedictine monk. It's a large tome, so stick to the poetic bits if you are pressed for time, like the paragraph in Chapter 17 which begins "Was ever another command so obeyed?" and which recounts the wonder of how the command of Jesus to make Eucharist has been faithfully obeyed by all sorts of people in all kinds of situations. It ends with these words: "week by week and month by month, on a hundred thousand successive Sundays, faithfully, unfailingly, across all the parishes of christendom, the pastors have done this just to make the *plebs sancta Dei*–the holy common people of God."[4]

While it is true that, as with the Divine Office, the initial vision faded for a time and the Eucharist decreased in frequency, especially during the eighteenth century, in the final analysis the Anglican tradition didn't do so badly. There were always those who kept the flame of the vision burning during the dark times (and ironically John Wesley was prime among them, earning the nickname of *methodist* for his frequent reception of Holy Communion when to do so was considered odd and extreme). It is doubtful whether things were managed better in the rest of the Western Church where the Mass was reduced to a public spectacle in which the faithful were normally excluded from communion.

In any event, within the Church of England, reinforcements were on their way. The Oxford Movement of the nineteenth century was followed in the 1930s by the Parish Communion Movement, which had wide appeal, promoting the concept of a Eucharist for the whole community around nine a.m., to be followed by a sit-down breakfast: heady stuff for those raised on a hole-in-the-corner approach to Communion at eight a.m. Although the breakfasts got simpler, the message stuck, and today there are few who would dispute the centrality of the Sunday Eucharist grounded both on Scripture and tradition. In all but the most extreme politically motivated parishes, the Eucharist is the norm for the main gathering of the liturgical assembly, Sunday by Sunday.

Alongside this centrality of the Eucharist, a particular benefit of the Anglican approach to worship has been a renewed emphasis on the Divine Office as the bread and butter of worship for the whole community of faith.

The Divine Office—the recitation of psalms, framed by antiphons and interspersed with readings—was first developed as a means of corporate prayer by Benedict (480–550), the father of monasticism in the Western Church. In time, the Divine Office was regularized into seven separate acts of worship (or "hours") during the day and one (Matins) during the night. The singing of the Divine Office was the trademark of the monastic houses of men and women consecrated to God by sacred vows.

Once again we owe a debt to Cranmer for releasing the Daily Office into the bloodstream of the Church. In the wake of the dissolution of the monastic houses of England in the 1530s, and in answer to the disappointing response to the availability of weekly Communion in the 1550s, it was Cranmer's brainwave to renew this structure of daily prayer by handing over the Divine Office to the whole people of God, simplifying it for popular consumption by cutting down the number of Offices to just two, for morning and evening. What had previously been the preserve of the cloister became the property of every parish church; what had previously been in Latin was now translated into English, and modern English at that.

It was a master-stroke by which the parish churches of England were provided with an invaluable tool for involving ordinary men and women in worship that actually meant something to them. Even the illiterate could for the first time (like the inhabitants of Jerusalem at the first Pentecost) "hear them telling in our own tongues the mighty works of God" (Acts 2:11). In this way, Cranmer hoped, "the people might continually profit more and more in the knowledge of God, and be the more inflamed with the love of his true religion."[5]

The saying together of Morning and Evening Prayer, day in, day out, for the last 450 years, by small groups of faithful Christians, has become the real bedrock of Anglican worship. In it the worshiper is united with the whole Church, past and present, in an offering of prayer that is, thanks to the time zones of the world, quite literally a seamless robe of unceasing praise. Although, as with all breathtakingly bold reforms, the flame of the original vision has flickered and faltered at times, nevertheless it has been kept burning, with great faithfulness and devotion.[6]

In the United States, the 1979 edition of the *Book of Common Prayer* provides four daily offices—morning, noon, evening, and night (compline)—that can be prayed in a variety of ways. Sung or recited in community or prayed silently by an individual, the Divine Office of the *BCP* contributes to the unity of the Church, in prayer, throughout the world.

In England, *Celebrating Common Prayer* has provided the Church with a rich and varied pattern for the Divine Office.[7] This has been produced in association with the Society of St. Francis, an Anglican religious community. Like so many of the very best things that the Church of England does, it is at present unofficial in that it was not commissioned by General Synod, yet it is used in literally thousands of churches and homes every day.

In recent decades this historic "basic kit" of Office and Eucharist has provided the "secure home background" for all kinds of experiments in worship, and this is wholly desirable.

The work of retranslating Eucharist and Office into contemporary language did not, of course, cease with the 1662 Prayer Book, although it remained the mainstay of Anglican worship for over three hundred years, despite all attempts to revise it. But the drive to make the language of worship intelligible to twentieth-century ears and hearts finally resulted in the publication, for the English Church, of *The Alternative Service Book 1980*, which, as its name implies, was only ever intended to be used alongside the Book of Common Prayer—and only for a limited period while the work of producing a new, permanent prayer book went on. The first part of *Common Worship*, a more definitive resource, was published in 2000, and is designed to be, rather than a book or books, a "collection of services and other liturgical material" both "rich and varied." Significantly, it is "published on the World Wide Web and through other electronic media as well as in print." Cranmer would have just *loved* it.

The process of liturgical reform is painstakingly slow in these more democratic times, when the more direct approach of Cranmer—who brooked no compromise with the traditionalists of his day—is no longer commended in classes on the management of change. The process familiar to us today, when progressives and conservatives lock horns over every jot and tittle of new texts, gives rise to compromises which satisfy no one and to a number of alternatives rather than a single solution.

The Episcopal Church, for example, still seems in a state of liturgical shock following its courageous "do or die" effort at reform in the 1970s. In 1979 the American Church, following many years of experimentation with several highly acclaimed provisional texts, beat the English to the punch with a complete new Book of Common Prayer. This was no mere alternative but a wholesale replacement of what had gone before, and this bold and admirable step seems to have exhausted the Episcopal Church. Apart from *Enriching our Worship* (1997), which was chiefly concerned with righting wrongs of exclusive language, no supplementary resources have been produced, and the work of liturgical renewal appears to have ground to a halt. By and large, Episcopalians remain book-bound in worship, more often than not managing to celebrate the "new" book in the "old" way, as if all that blood, sweat and tears in 1979 were to no avail.

As with ecumenism, however, it may well be that hope for renewal of worship will come from below, not above. The church planting movement has shown us the potential of eucharistic worship that is stripped down to its bare bones and celebrated in all kinds of hired premises as a sign of the pilgrim church making its journey alongside the unchurched. This is not only an evangelistic insight (with a dramatically successful track record), but a liberating experience of worship of great joy, simplicity and immediacy, in which the basic components of liturgy are rediscovered.[8]

Today, in the new missionary situation of the Western world at the beginning of the third millennium, much more will be required of us in the risk-taking business. That is why you are likely to stumble across a whole host of non-liturgical forms of worship—from pram services to all-night raves—which it is important to respect for the evangelistic motives that lie behind it. Late-night services in cathedrals—all flickering candles, mood music and incense—are but one example of the experimental worship services springing up everywhere to cater for the countless hosts who, perceiving the Church as irrelevant, nevertheless seek a spirituality rather than a religion (a message not so very far from that of Jesus).

This is an exciting time to be discovering liturgy, as we begin to loosen up a little after centuries of living in compartments, to allow ourselves to feed from the well-stocked storehouses of other traditions. In this way the boundaries become blurred and our prejudices a little less sharp. Taizé is but one example of this process, a Protestant community with a Catholic style, evolving worship with which the whole world feels at home and to which young people, impatient with the stuffiness of the churches, flock in their tens of thousands.

Impatience is something we could do with a little more of in our churches right now. The treasures of the Anglican storehouse have served to make us liturgically fat and complacent, and as you venture out into the great Anglican unknown, you will need great determination to keep going. Although, of course, there are glorious exceptions in every diocese, the experience of liturgical worship in the average parish can be abysmal. While the departed glories of the past are still hankered after, the demands of the present are ignored and the challenges of the future derided because they are feared. Time and time again, a handful of elderly people (with the under-sixties forming the crèche) are found to have hijacked the local church, commandeered the hymn-list and vetoed change, thereby repelling all boarders. The clergy who connive at such tricks, and stand aside pathetically wringing their hands in mock exasperation, should be given early retirement, no matter what the cost, as a matter of priority in the Church's mission strategy.

Thankfully, there are signs that the Spirit is moving and that we are finding the courage to start again, addressing the imbalances of the Reformation era–the suppression of movement, art and imagery in worship, arising from the reformers' own hang-ups with past excesses–and feeling free to use everything that is good and true, no matter how unlikely the source.

The liturgical insights of the present Christian era, insights shared by every tradition in every continent, are those that recall us above all to our community life around the table of the Lord. This is no more a "whim" than the Reformation was a "whim"; it is what the Spirit is saying to the churches today. "The faithful community must be brought to the recognition of itself in liturgy."[9]

There is no reason at all why in this rediscovered emphasis on the immanent and the communal we should lose for one moment the sense of mystery and transcendence. It all depends on how much trouble we take, and the Anglican tradition prompts us to take a great deal of trouble. When Anglicans get it right, it is very good indeed; intimate and awe-inspiring, dignified and joyful, structured and with room for spontaneity–a taste of heaven, no less.

Above all, the Anglican tradition will give you an experience of worship *in community*: alien to our way of doing things is the vast, impersonal throng, in which one simply goes through the religious motions, chalking up another attendance statistic. With us you will be recognized and known, welcomed and (after a little while, because we're shy) appreciated, and (eventually, because we're of English stock and slow in coming forward) your particular gifts discerned and made use of. It may take some time, but in the end you will feel as if you've come home.

So don't give up hope, and keep exploring. Find out what's going on and where; investigate with an open heart and mind, and take to yourself that which is good, and honest, and beautiful, and true. In that way will the Anglican tradition of worship be kept alive, venturing forth from known positions to encounter God afresh on the edges of our experience. In change and renewal shall we be most faithful to the tradition of the Church (and to the insights of Cranmer), and thus continue to build up patterns of worship of incomparable richness and diversity.

10 Learning Good Habits
The Anglican Approach to Prayer

This chapter may end up being the shortest, simply because it will be the hardest to write. First of all, prayer is simply *hard*. You never seem to be able to make the time, you never know what to say, and it can seem that there's never anybody in when you call. Priests' studies may be lined with books *about* prayer, but they will probably be the first to admit that knowing any amount of theory doesn't get you very far; the actual business of praying is another thing altogether. Secondly, the all-inclusive nature of the Anglican Communion means that the experience of prayer in our tradition is incredibly varied and almost impossible to categorize.

Reflecting the wide and colorful spectrum of Anglican ecclesiology referred to in Chapter Seven, the picture conjured up by the mere mention of the word *prayer* can mean anything from a deliverance ministry in a charismatic prayer group, to contemplative prayer in an enclosed convent, with choral evensong in a cathedral setting somewhere in between.

Until fairly recently, it might have been said that the basic Anglican approach to prayer was low-key, pragmatic and with a reluctance to expect too much. For most it was a hard slog, with the good old British stiff upper lip coming in very handy. Two developments in recent decades have changed this picture quite significantly, and the whole question is suddenly more interesting.

To use a dietary analogy, my parents' generation grew up knowing only an unremitting diet of "solid English food." Dining out was an unheard-of activity, and the very idea of foreign food quite unthinkable. Changing social patterns and holidays abroad have given my own generation a quite different attitude, and to experience different foods from different cultures is now part and parcel of everyday life for all sectors of society, whether in posh restaurants or from food trucks on street corners.

Let's begin with the basic fare, thinking of the historic pattern of liturgical prayer–Office and Eucharist–as the solid Anglican food which has sustained us over the centuries. Later, we will turn to the spiritual equivalent of the two dishes which have most revolutionized our eating habits–the hot Indian curry and French *nouvelle cuisine*. The previous notes on worship will have given you a few clues about the Anglican love of dignity and order and understatement in liturgy, and the same goes for prayer generally.

Although traditionally great store is set by personal prayer as the foundation of all that we do together, Anglicans can get quite defensive about prayer as a "private matter," so it is very difficult to assess exactly what is going on in the home as a place where a prayer life is nurtured and exercised. The signs are not encouraging; the increasingly frantic timetables of most families make the simple giving of thanks before meals, let alone a short time of reflection together, less and less common. Even for the individual to carve out a few minutes quiet in a normal, healthy (= crazy) household is virtually impossible, and the privacy of the bathroom is not always the most conducive environment for heavenly thoughts.

J. L. Carr, in his novel *The Harpole Report*, recounts the story of the teacher who proudly claimed twenty years' experience in a particular school, only to be corrected that she had in fact only had the same experience twenty times. Unless continually renewed by our life together in the community of faith, our own personal prayer can deteriorate to the level of that poor teacher's experience of education; not a journey of constant exploration, but a continual reiteration, day in day out, of the same few words learned years ago at confirmation class or even Sunday school.

For these reasons, we as Anglicans know our great need of each other when it comes to prayer. No one is better placed than the parish priest to realize how one's prayer life is so easily eaten away by the phone call as one is leaving the house, the conversation that it seems so important to continue, the cry for help that no one could refuse. For that reason, the clergy know full well that the Daily Office is their only hope of retaining any prayer life at all, the discipline of being in a certain place at a certain time where others will meet with you in mutual dependence in prayer.

Most of our praying is therefore done together—at the Eucharist or Daily Office in church or in the house group at home—and we realize only too well our need of being carried by others, especially at times when we feel dry or despairing. The Gospel story of the paralyzed man let down into the presence of Jesus by his friends is not a bad image to hang onto.

Participation in the liturgy reminds us that prayer is not just for Christmas but for keeps; not restricted to the times we feel in the mood or need something desperately, but every day, every week, without fail.

By praying together we help one another learn good habits of prayer, and hopefully our praying spills over into the rest of our lives, even if it's only mumbling to God in the car as we crawl to work. Through praying together we are given something to chew on when we chat to God, recalling moments together in the community of faith, the phrases used, the refrains sung.

Typically, Anglicans award high marks for presentation. We like things to be done well, and prayed well, with beautiful language uttered mellifluously in musical cadences with an ear finely tuned for the dramatic pause. At the same time we prize sincerity and an appropriate humility when addressing the Almighty, scorning the meticulous enunciations of the pompous cathedral canon as much as the vacuous repetitions of the over-familiar prayer group member, sprawled cross-legged in an easy chair.

We like praying that is sincere but not over-earnest, inspired but not ostentatious, and we are easily embarrassed by others making fools of themselves. We try to be faithful to the advice of Jesus on the subject (Matt. 6:6–14), being quite keen on prayer as a private affair (v. 6) and quite definitely not keen on "heaping up empty phrases" (v. 7). On the whole we are gentle and unpretentious in our praying, valuing regular routine rather than religious zeal.

Traditionally, the Anglican instinct is to go for set prayers composed by others, trusting, with typical deference, the experience and wisdom of "the all-time greats" rather than one's own stumbling and stammering efforts. I still remember now the framed copy of the prayer of that old soldier of Christ, St. Ignatius Loyola, which hung on the bedroom wall above my grandmother's bed, and which I came to know by heart as a child:

> Teach me good Lord, to give and not to count the cost, to fight and not to heed the wounds, to toil and not to seek for rest, to labor and not to ask for any reward, save that of knowing that we do your will.

Later on, the second collect at Morning Prayer was one I used to recite to myself between the bus stop and the school gates, just in case the classroom bully was in energetic form. It was called the Collect for Peace, of which I felt greatly in need at the time:

> O God, who art the author of peace and lover of concord, in knowledge of whom standeth our eternal life, whose service is perfect freedom; Defend us thy humble servants in all assaults of our enemies; that we, surely trusting in thy defense, may not fear the power of any adversaries, through the might of Jesus Christ our Lord.

Provided we remember the cautionary tale of J. L. Carr's teacher, and constantly seek to spread our wings, familiar and much-loved prayers such as these, repeated over and over again, can be extremely effective at calming nerves and soothing the soul, and as Anglicans we have readily available to us more than our fair share of absolute winners which, if you take the trouble to learn one or two by heart, will be found true friends in time of pray-er's block.

Cranmer's matchless collection of prayers retained in the 1662 Book of Common Prayer is justly renowned as a priceless treasure. Many were brand new creations of the period, while others were culled from a surprisingly wide range of sources. These included translations from the Latin of the Sarum Rite, that quarry of liturgical goodies originating at Salisbury Cathedral but in general use across England by the eve of the Reformation, and more exotically, adaptations from the revised breviary of the Spanish Cardinal Francisco de Quinones, commissioned by none other than Pope Paul III, Henry VIII's bitter enemy. Cranmer knew quality when he saw it, and didn't hesitate to poach where appropriate, whatever the source. This was entirely in keeping with the Anglican instinct to break new ground while at the same time carefully maintaining continuity with the best of all that had gone before.

Called *collects* because they collected the themes of the day and the thoughts of the faithful into one short prayer at the beginning of the Eucharist, these prayers came to symbolize and encapsulate the approach to God typical of Anglicanism. They were learned parrot-fashion in schools and confirmation classes, so that phrases from them became embedded in English usage, with an application far beyond the confines of church life. They became part of our culture. Here is a typical example, and a favorite of mine; the collect for the Sixth Sunday after Trinity in the 1662 Book of Common Prayer, first translated from the Latin of the Sarum Missal in the 1549 book:

> O God, who hast prepared for them that love thee
> such good things as pass man's understanding:
> Pour into our hearts such love towards thee, that
> we, loving thee above all things, may obtain thy
> promises, which exceed all that we can desire;
> through Jesus Christ our Lord.

Here is a prayer you can savor, ponder on and chew over and never exhaust its possibilities: a prayer worth praying. What's more, to enjoy it you no longer have to flounder amid the archaisms of sixteenth- and seventeenth-century language, for these prayers have been redrafted and further improved in subsequent revisions of the original prayer books: *The Alternative*

Service Book 1980 and *Celebrating Common Prayer* (1992). So, for example, in 1980 the above collect was transposed to the Last Sunday after Pentecost (then the new classification for "ordinary" Sundays not falling within a particular liturgical season), and was rewritten in contemporary language, with God now addressed as "merciful" (a characteristic of the Godhead perhaps necessary as never before in view of our dithering on liturgical reform?)

It is often the case, however, that mere translations from Tudor into contemporary English end up sounding trite and lifeless. Nothing could better illustrate the need to always keep a look-out for gems in unlikely places than the emergence of the collects from the 1997 Sacramentary from the International Commission for English Texts. This collection of new collects crafted from the themes of the Sunday readings is simply matchless, leaving our Prayer Book alternatives looking limp and lifeless. Sadly, the Vatican found them a little *too* creative for its liking, and so Anglicans, following behind the delivery truck, have picked up an incredibly valuable cast-off. These prayers should be savored and used widely.[1]

On the debit side, our reliance on set forms has left us rather tongue-tied in this "second age of the Spirit," when Christians of every tradition are becoming more at home with free, unstructured prayer. Anglicans might well be heard declining an invitation to open a meeting with prayer simply because they "haven't brought their book" with them, and going back to our dietary analogy, this is where we come to the spiritual equivalent of the two new culinary delights which have revolutionized our way of eating.

The hot Indian curry which has spiced up our prayer life in the Anglican Communion in recent decades, and which is now available on practically every street corner, is the dynamic experience of charismatic prayer, in which God is experienced afresh, interested and involved in the smallest details of our life: a person to whom we can address our every concern and need and who can act with power, directness and immediacy. Significantly, this hot food can be taken sitting in the restaurant or can be taken away for home consumption.

It is an explosive concoction which cannot be contained within pew or prayer book. The good news about it is that the days of prayer as a hard slog are over; we are no longer expected to struggle through set forms, but actually to *enjoy* it as it equips us for the Christian journey with a new sense of confidence in a God who can do anything. By and large, the Evangelical wing of the Church has taken to this spicy food in a big way, and as a result has been renewed and energized. Furthermore, the Renewal Movement (the movement that started out as the Charismatic Renewal during the 1960s) has watered all parts of the Anglican garden to some extent, blurring the edges of the old, rigid ways of doing things, giving us all a new, more relaxed approach to prayer and teaching us a few new tunes with which to sing the Lord's song. Today, the ability (if not the preference) to pray extempore is regarded as part of the basic kit of ministry, irrespective of tradition. In a complementary development of mutual upbuilding, printed collections of treasured prayers are more widely used than ever. "Political praying" (addressing God in language and forms decreed by a particular party or movement) is largely a thing of the past.

The Renewal Movement is characterized by an exuberance and freedom in prayer and corporate worship, a renewed sense of direct access to God recalling the Church to the period described in the Acts of the Apostles, with high expectations of healings, speaking in tongues, prophecy and other signs and wonders revealing God's direct intervention in our ordinary affairs. Even if a waning of the initial ecstatic period can be observed, the Renewal Movement has achieved immeasurable good in loosening up the Church, causing us to pray and to express our love for God with less inhibition and awkwardness, the name of Jesus more often on our lips. Interestingly, even though the 1960s leading lights of this movement came from the States (Dennis Bennett and Graham and Betty Pulkingham), their influence was felt in England more than in their home country (where I suppose prophets have always had a hard time).

There is, however, a second and quite different culinary delight which has had widespread influence: French *nouvelle cuisine*. Its equivalent for us is the radical approach to prayer, which is minimalist in style, taking us back to basics and to a fearless reappraisal, in the light of experience and of world events, of what we imagine is happening when we pray. In this process, we discard as far as possible all the jargon collected over two thousand years, and translate the meaning of God into our own language. (And the fact that this pulls us in the opposite direction to charismatic prayer only serves to make the whole subject more interesting–it's just as well we're Anglicans!) Thus, Bishop David Jenkins, in a talk given in 1967,[2] described the two foci of prayer as worship–"the response to the supremely valuable, ultimately transcendent personalness who is God," and grace–"the awareness . . . of the presence of an otherness which gives resources beyond one's own."

Whereas there are countless Anglicans who can exult in God's triumphant power at work in the world, there are others (who knows how many because no one quite dares own up) who are uneasy with the notion of a God who can, after earnest prayer, heal an individual's toothache, but who apparently remains powerless or unconcerned with the fate of six million of his specially chosen people in the Holocaust.

In other words, "God as an interventionist does not cut any ice,"[3] and to suppose that God responds only in some cases and not in others makes it even worse, for then God appears to be a moody and capricious tyrant. Intercession is therefore a real problem, and perhaps somewhere along the line we have got hold of the wrong end of the stick, approaching God in prayer like children with a list for Santa Claus rather than as adults content simply to bask in God's presence. This may help us grow into prayer defined by Christopher Scott as "allowing my being to become in tune with Being itself."[4] This may sound a bit New Age for our liking, but it's probably what Jesus was busy doing when he went off alone into solitary places, getting away from the disciples so that he could enjoy the company of his Father. Certainly we have no hint of shopping-list praying from Jesus. In the one prayer he taught us, the only request is for sufficient daily sustenance, and this is set firmly within a framework of praise to the holy God revealed as Father. When, before his arrest, he did plead earnestly for his own rescue, the answer was *no*. Or was that Gethsemane prayer a cry of human need which Jesus would not normally have graced with the name of prayer? Perhaps he expected no answer, for his life-long unity with the source of all being meant that he already sensed the shape of things to come.

There are of course many other nourishing dishes available in addition to these two already described in some detail. All the renewal movements of Anglican history contribute to the offering of a rich feast of prayer. While the Evangelical gives us a fresh appreciation of simplicity and sincerity born of an awareness of God's mercy and grace, the Catholic never allows us to imagine we are alone when we pray, pointing us to the unseen host of prayer-partners which is the Communion of Saints. We are not talking here of course of praying *to* the saints, but of asking them to pray *with* us, which seems a pretty natural thing to do if we believe that "death has no more dominion over us" and that "dead" fellow-Christians are as alive (indeed probably more alive) than those we see around us and whose prayers we request.

It is to the Catholic movement also that we owe the restoration of the Religious Life (communities of women or men consecrated to God by life-long vows) after a gap of three hundred years following Henry VIII's closure of all Religious Houses in England. Women led the way (in the 1840s this was the only opening for full-time service available to them), and today in the Church of England over sixty different Religious Communities provide oases of prayer, and remind us of the many ways of prayer, developed by the saints over the centuries, into which we can tap here and now. There really was no need for the Beatles to have gone all that way to India . . . the Church has known about meditation for a very long time (though perhaps we've kept it too much of a good secret). Today, the Indian sub-continent has come to us, in the shape of the dramatic growth in the proportion of our population of Asian origin, and if present trends in birth rates continue, Muslims will outnumber Christians in the United Kingdom in the foreseeable future. At the same time, rampant Western materialism eats away at spirituality in all its forms.

In the face of these developments, we need to display renewed confidence, not by banging the Christian drum, but by taking the lead in exploring ways in which all those in the West who seek God can learn, if only to a limited extent, to pray together. The Muslim's submission to the will of God, and the Buddhist's self-surrender to the Infinite, can teach us a lot, and even help redress the balance of Christian prayer, which is all too often centered on self rather than God, and couched in terms of theological imperialism rather than humble attentiveness.

Nevertheless, Anglicans do not think of themselves as exercising a dominant role in the world's praying. We plod along on the beat rather than rushing around amidst the glitz of the International Prayer Squad, but we get the job done. Our big names are not in the same league as Teresa of Avila or Catherine of Siena, but are gentle hermits like Richard Rolle, godly bishops like Lancelot Andrewes, passionate lovers like John Donne, scholarly mystics like Thomas Treherne, or country parsons like George Herbert. In our own generation, R. S. Thomas kept the priest-poet tradition burning fierce and bright from his parish amidst the wild beauty of the Lleyn Peninsula, where on sleepless nights, listening to the sea, he thinks

> of that other being who is awake, too,
> letting our prayers break over him,
> not like this for a few hours,
> but for days, years, for eternity.[5]

Above all, Anglicans tend not to get too hung up about structures and formularies of prayer, preferring to "chat to the boss" whenever and wherever it is possible, engaging him in polite but relaxed conversation. In this way we aim to develop a prayer life that becomes second nature to us, and in the end (and this usually takes a whole lifetime) is as natural as breathing.

Robert Llewellyn likens prayer to children at play; they don't realize they are playing, they are just getting on with doing it.[6] They do not need to be interrupted to have what they are doing analyzed or explained to them; that would kill their play stone dead. This picture appeals very much to the Anglican mind. We'd like to think that in getting on with doing it, rather than thinking about it, and in fostering a naturalness in our relationship with God that is neither craven nor casual, we have got it just about right.

Lord, in your mercy, hear our prayer.

Checks and Balances

The Anglican Approach to Authority

John V. Taylor, Bishop of Winchester in the 1980s, considered that exercise of authority in the Anglican tradition was "like taking a large collection of dogs for a walk in the country without enough leads."[1]

Certainly, Anglicanism is often caricatured as an out-of-control conglomeration of individualists doing their own thing, but although we all long for a little more authority from time to time (usually when tiresome people seem to be getting away with it), on the whole we believe that the Anglican balance between central structure and local responsibility is about right. The problem is that it is very difficult to determine how the Christian Church should be governed (What on earth would God do with the Church? we might well ask), even if we had a free hand to start all over again.

Despite the blood, sweat and tears expended down the centuries, all attempts to establish indisputable scriptural if not divine authority for this or that theory of Church government and structure remain contentious. It is increasingly questioned whether Jesus himself had much interest in structuring his disciples into a recognizable and separate entity which in due course could come to be known as the Church.

For Jesus, authority lay in the will of God, and God's will was discerned by those who gave God absolute obedience, not merely by keeping a set of organizational rules, but by going beyond the rules to live God-filled lives. Final authority lay in the one single absolute of love, even to the extent of laying down one's life for one's friends. Furthermore, Jesus of Nazareth reserved his most severe condemnation for any form of religious structure or pressure group that got in the way of this new relationship with God.

The first Christian communities are interesting prototypes for modern churches to study and learn from, but even they were living in a world different from ours. Although it is hard for us in mainstream churches to imagine how anyone could have got away with the authoritarianism exercised by Paul as described by the writer of Acts, don't forget that an autocratic leadership is alive and well today at either end of the ecclesial spectrum. Some storefront church pastors could tell the Pope a thing or two about absolute power.

We often think of Paul as an ecclesiastical version of a U.S. marshal stamping law and order on tension-ridden townships of the Wild West. A little reading between the lines reveals that things were far from being that clear-cut among the first Christian communities of the eastern Mediterranean. One indication that things easily went awry is that those who followed Paul felt it necessary to be economical with the truth by attributing to him letters they themselves had written in an attempt to crack down on indiscipline and abuse of power.[2] Neither Paul nor his followers were averse to frequent readings of the riot act, and we can safely say that the "thorn in the flesh" referred to by Paul (2 Cor. 12:7) was not over-frequent meetings of his local church council. Democracy was an aberration to be reserved for the twentieth century.

Those first Christian communities were development corporations rather than local authorities, provisional pioneering bodies supervising the injection of substantial amounts of capital into new areas of growth. Development corporations in England[3] have proven themselves incredibly successful agencies for putting in place the infrastructure that will enable new balanced and vibrant communities to grow and prosper, but we don't want them to go on forever. We become uneasy about unelected bodies having so much power, and sooner or later the agitation begins for government by locally elected representatives. The fact that the local authorities may not be able to do the job half as well is seen as beside the point, for such transition of power represents an inevitable development in Western democratic societies.

So it is with the Church. The first communities were pioneers in a provisional phase of development spiritually financed by the injection of substantial amounts of Holy Spirit. Those were heady days, and if you'd like a taste of how things were, seek out a copy of the *Didache*, the earliest Christian text outside the New Testament, and earlier than the four Gospels.[4] The *Didache* recalls a primitive stage of development when traveling missionaries and prophets held sway, and when bishops had yet to be distinguished from presbyters. Subsequent developments saw the Church having to settle down to respectability, coming to terms with an emphasis on maintenance rather than mission. Of course, there was no question then of increased democratization, but nevertheless the balance between central authority and local responsibility gradually shifted toward the latter, albeit in the shape of feudal lords who gradually obtained the right to nominate to the bishop the priests who would care for the parishes in their domain.

Ever since 312, when the Roman Empire adopted Christianity as the State religion, and the Church accepted State protection and a privileged position in society, the Church has found itself severely hampered in exercising a purely spiritual authority over its membership. Over the centuries, deals had to be made and compromises arrived at in order for the Church to survive under all kinds of secular regimes, many of them indifferent if not antagonistic to the Christian cause. All this weakened the power and influence of the Church as a centralized ecclesiastical authority, and it was at times reduced to a subservient role in the face of secular domination.

As we have already seen, in the twelfth century Henry II was responsible not only for the death of Thomas Becket but also for his previous appointment as Archbishop and his exile for six of his eight years in office. In the sixteenth century, Henry VIII's attempts to prevail upon Pope Clement VII to annul his marriage to Catherine of Aragon were foiled, not by spiritual authority faithfully and dispassionately exercised, but by spiritual authority in the thrall of a secular power, Charles V, the Holy Roman Emperor. Crime boss Henry Tudor found himself up against a bigger and more powerful Mafia dynasty, one which provided the Pope's operation with better protection. Charles V, the Holy Roman Emperor, was a much bigger fish than the English king, and was not a man for the Pope to cross needlessly.

By an ironic twist of fate, the Emperor's niece happened to be none other than Catherine of Aragon, so Henry, arguing a difficult case to start with, found his goose well and truly cooked by this fateful combination of religious and political factors. It has ever been thus in the Church after Constantine.

The highly centralized and authoritarian structure which is the Roman Catholic Church of today, and increasingly so, is a relatively recent phenomenon. Many features of this impressive structure owe their origin to the nineteenth-century Ultramontane movement, which sought to restore the glories of the past and elevate the papacy at the expense of national interests and even of episcopacy itself. In this, modern technology has joined hands with Curial ambition to create a centralized power base that medieval popes could not even have dreamt of, in which emasculated bishops find themselves wondering whether the much-heralded collegiality of Vatican II was just a mirage.

All this needs to be said to set the Anglican experience in the context of Church history throughout Europe. We may not be very good at centralized authority, but others' experience tells us that we shouldn't be. There's no need for us Anglicans to hang our heads in shame because we don't have an ecclesiastical version of the secret police to ensure conformity to the party line. Our naiveté in these matters should be a source of pride. Amazingly, and perhaps by accident rather than design, we have once again come up with an answer that works well and that gives us a right balance between head office and local branch, between Church and church.

The Archbishop of Canterbury is senior pastor of our Communion, because his office has been around a long time (Rowan Williams is the 104th occupant of the see, Augustine first opening the store in 597. Note that, with our vivid sense of continuity with the Pre-Reformation Church, we count from Augustine, not from some poor benighted Tudor prelate). The Archbishop of Canterbury does not, however, rule over a centralized worldwide body. He has neither curia nor Swiss Guard, and is hardly ever seen in a white cassock (except perhaps on a very hot day in Tanzania). Like the Ecumenical Patriarch of Constantinople, chief pastor of the Orthodox Churches, he bears the honorable and ancient title *primus inter pares*–first among equals–as a model of leadership in the Church as originally understood. In this, once again the Anglican Communion's way of doing things resonates with the tradition of the Eastern Church. The later development of a monarchical papacy, which happened in the Western Church, has no part in either of our traditions.

Of course, there is a price to pay. Our bishops are sometimes an embarrassment, and we can be left feeling shortchanged in the matter of apostolic authority exercised with unfaltering élan. At worst, the primary episcopal virtue seems to be that of not rocking the boat (rather than navigating it), with the ability to act the entertainment officer coming in a close second. Being a bishop in the United States is a particularly thankless task, for in the Episcopal Church the balance of power (in an unhealthy and un-Anglican way) leans heavily toward the local parish, with the bishop forced to exercise authority mostly by smiling a lot.

It may seem a little archaic for English bishops to sign themselves by the name of their see (Rowan Cantuar, David Ebor, etc.), but seen from the American side of the pond, there are distinct advantages in emphasizing the see rather than the individual, the chair rather than its occupant. In the Episcopal Church the bishop is usually referred to by his second name (Bishop Smith will be with us next Sunday), and addressed as such liturgically: "Bishop Smith we present to you . . ." In England it would tend to be "Our Bishop will be with us next Sunday" and liturgically "Right Reverend Father in God we present to you . . ."

These anachronisms enshrine a crucial understanding of Catholic order: that the bishop is important for the *office*, not the person. In England we may like our bishop, or we may despair of him, but that's hardly relevant. Even with the availability of "flying bishops" for the disaffected, the diocesan bishop remains the bishop, like it or lump it.

In the United States, the cult of personality among bishops is alive and well, and the office of the bishop is diminished as a consequence. Horror stories abound of American clergy who organize theological lynch mobs to interrogate chief pastors as to their views on the atonement or the resurrection. Obedience, and the paying of the parish pledge, can thus be made conditional upon the bishop's performance: a wonderful scam for the arrogant and the self-righteous to avoid their responsibilities. But this is nothing new: Our Lord had exactly the same problem with the Pharisees who found religious reasons for dishonoring their parents (Mark 7:11).

We can perhaps smile (if we don't cry) at the irony that the province of the Anglican Communion that bears the name *Episcopal* should be the least episcopal in practice. All that being said, we tend to believe that imbalances of this kind are a price worth paying for the freedom to be ourselves, and to live in an atmosphere unclouded by fear or by attempts to quench the Spirit.

"Head Office" for Anglicans tends to be an amorphous mass of ill-defined institutions and symbolic figures dressed up to the nines, hovering somewhere between Westminster Abbey and Washington National Cathedral—an amalgam of splendid liturgies in awesome spaces, measured debates in synod or convention, and efficient bureaucrats beavering away in Millbank SW1 or at 815 Second Avenue, New York City. All this spells *church* with a capital *C*, at which level we can see clearly the Anglican penchant for checks and balances, which maintains not only a desirable equilibrium but also (unless we are very careful) a stultifying status quo.

In the twentieth century the whole machinery of Church government was made more accountable with the creation of democratic structures of conventions (United States) and synods

(England). In this process the American Church, not surprisingly, led the way, though astonishingly it excluded women from the legislative process until 1970. The Anglican Communion is a family of churches for whom episcopacy—that is, government by bishops—is the essential element of their common life. At every level of the Church we have therefore a delicate balance of power between episcopal authority and legislative assembly: between the bishops, whom everyone imagines to be more powerful than they really are, and the synods, or convention, which everyone imagines to be less powerful than they really are. The bishops and clergy may manage the shop and chat up the customers, but the synods grind away in the back room, keeping the business plan firmly under their control.

At the national level, the House of Bishops forms the consecrated hierarchy to whom the people in the parishes look for a lead, and to whom they feel they can relate better than to a committee or a bureaucracy. At the same time the House of Bishops is but one out of three houses of the synod or convention (alongside Clergy and Laity), each of which must approve any legislative measure put before it to achieve its implementation. Bishops on both sides of the Atlantic have tended to collude in the increasing devolution of power to council and committee, stifling initiative and hampering creative reform and the disposition of manpower. Fortunately, most of this passes over the head of the average person-in-the-check-out-queue, who probably thinks that on the whole it's rather nice to be part of something big and impressive, even if the hem is sagging on the best embroidered cope, and the crowds don't turn out on the streets as they used to do.

When we come to the diocese, the area under the jurisdiction of a bishop, we see the same balance of power at work between the diocesan bishop as chief pastor, and the diocesan synod or convention. The synod or convention of a diocese is made up of clergy and lay members elected or appointed (methods vary in different provinces) to debate and legislate on matters of major importance affecting the Church. All this sounds excellent stuff, but these bodies, made up, for the most part, of good, honest, and open-minded people, are vulnerable to those individuals or groups whose lives are reduced to a single issue and who have an obsessive love for axe-grinding. This does mean of course that at this level a creative bishop has more of a fighting chance to effect change and implement his vision, a degree of maneuverability essential if the bishop is to be in any sense a prophet as well as a priest. Sometimes—just sometimes—a skilled and creative bishop can energize a synod or convention to effect radical change or provide fresh vision, but in this setting prophetic leadership is no easy task, and accordingly, extremely rare.

The bishop (or *overseer* in the New Testament) symbolizes our corporate life as Anglicans in a particular diocese, and through his/her fellow bishops links us to all our sister communities across the world. Bishops today are burdened with high expectations and a great deal of loyalty and affection, but such are the demands of simply keeping the show on the road that they find themselves hamstrung in implementing radical programs for change. This of course presupposes a desire for change, and it can be argued that the checks, balances and endless consultation surrounding episcopal appointments have made bold, creative, strategic thinking even more of a rarity than it was. The diocesan bishop is assisted in most cases by a suffragan bishop or two, the dean of the cathedral, and (in England) by archdeacons or (in the U.S.) a canon to the ordinary. Together with heads of departments, this group forms the bishop's staff meeting—the think-tank responsible for the day-to-day running of the diocese.

There are one hundred dioceses in the United States, forty-four in England, and thirty in Canada. Some of them are ridiculously large, thereby depriving their people of effective and authentic episcopal oversight not rectified by gaggles of area bishops. England has been thinking about creating another province or two since AD 735, and America (despite the creation of "paper provinces") doesn't seem to have considered the devolution of power at all, such is its innate fear of anything archepiscopal. The United States can, however, be credited with the admirable tradition of coadjutor bishops—bishops elected before the retirement of the diocesan but with the right of succession, enabling them to learn on the job alongside their predecessor. Coadjutors have never caught on in the Church of England, although they are also a feature of the Roman Communion.

Suffragan bishops are part of the ecclesiastical scenery on both sides of the Atlantic, and serve as bishop assistants to diocesans with large populations to care for. In England they get a slightly better deal, with a named see of their own, but either way they represent a typical Anglican fudging of the issue. Why go to the trouble of making episcopacy really *work* with small manageable dioceses when you can put off the evil day by simply appointing yet another suffragan to prop up the creaking house?

No bishop can remain an island, and all at times need minders, bouncers and henchmen to keep the unruly kids in line and to do the dirty work. In the United Kingdom this task is performed by the archdeacons (at least two per diocese), who care for a geographical sub-division of a diocese and deal with the nitty-gritty issues. In England (as you might expect) the archdeacon is never a deacon, but in the United States he or she often is. Here the name is used differently to describe someone who has pastoral care of the deacons in a diocese, one of their number being elevated to class monitor.

The U.S. equivalent of an archdeacon is the canon to the ordinary: a presbyter with some clout who is the bishop's Man or Woman Friday, and who plays nasty cop when the two of them go down to a parish where something unpleasant has just been found in the woodshed. Each diocese is sub-divided into deaneries—a cluster of between ten and twenty parishes—each served by its own synod or plenary meeting. Because we haven't yet worked out what a deanery really is or should be, and because we have extracted all the teeth from the area dean's role (not that there were any in the first place), deanery synods or plenaries tend to be talking shops often avoided by the more dynamic of the Church's members.

At parish level we see again the delicate balance in play between episcopally authorized leader and legislative council. The oversight of each parish is delegated by the bishop to a parish priest, who is given authority over the local church but who works alongside the people of God, not lording it over them. Although the "cure of souls" gives the priest a great deal of freedom of movement in matters spiritual and liturgical, he or she exercises authority in partnership with the parochial church council (England) or vestry (United States), whose backing must be secured for any major change in parish life as well as in matters of finance.

In England the parish priest (rector or vicar), on being installed in a parish, has usually been granted the freehold possession of the benefice, which means in effect that he or she cannot be ousted unless something goes very seriously wrong. Moreover, the priest can continue in office up to the age of seventy.

Security of tenure is somewhat more precarious for clergy in the U.S. because it is the vestry that hires and fires, albeit in consultation with the bishop. Wherever there is a mismatch, the priest can very easily be made to feel the hireling rather than the shepherd, and his/her position can become untenable. Needless to say, this is a system not conducive to prophetic voices, and there are parishes where you could imagine a head on a platter being required before anyone sat up and took notice.

Conversely, the situation in England can lead to parish clergy overstaying their welcome (or at least their sell-by date) by many years, crushing the life out of a parish by dint of much "vain repetition" of ideas let alone sermons. Imagine for just a moment, furthermore, any organization in which a branch manager, no matter how inefficient, downright lazy or barking mad, was a fixture for life (even when his branch had practically collapsed around him), and you will realize why the Church cannot afford this luxury for very much longer. Unless we can develop ordained leaders ready to serve where they are needed, secure in their role and yet accountable, all our talk of strategic planning and renewal of the structure is exposed as mere play-acting.

Meanwhile, back at the ranch, we will, hopefully, find the parish priest hard at work, assisted by two lay wardens, elected by the annual meeting of the parish (though clergy retain certain nomination rights, especially if they have their wits about them), whose first priority is to work closely with the priest for the good of the parish. They will be supported by the other members of the parochial church council or vestry, and in our more healthy parishes there is a growing emphasis on collaborative ministry, with a large degree of delegation to ministry teams of various kinds. The days of the one-man or one-woman show are over.

As usual in Anglicanism, the system allows you to make of it what you will. The balance of power can swing wildly between clergy and people; in some parishes the priest hides under the table at the wardens' approach, in others, by sheer force of personality, he or she gets away with murder. But to talk of clergy and laity as two distinct or even opposing camps is really old hat; the best priests are those who are eroding the distinctions in order to build local Christian communities in which ministry is shared by all those willing to give the necessary commitment.

Much could be done to erase hierarchical distinctions within the Christian body if clergy lived just a little more dangerously, being more creative about rituals in worship which make the empowerment of the laity visible and understandable, and being more reckless in letting go of the clerical collar. One disappointment at the ordination of women is that sadly they have not helped us to rethink what it means to be a presbyter in the Church of God in today's world, and to re-model how it looks and operates. Their enthusiasm to simply join the men's club on the old terms is, while perfectly understandable, a missed opportunity for all of us. But I digress.

Underlying all these checks and balances at various levels is the principle of episcopacy, although, as we have seen, with our track record of failing to redraw provincial and diocesan boundaries, we seem at times to be doing our best to make it unworkable. I feel I must apologize for my church at this point, but for every apology you will find a hundred champions of the status quo with a thousand plausible reasons for doing nothing, reasons which mask failure of vision and loss of nerve.

Episcopacy is important to get right because Anglicans believe that, although no one really has a clue as to what really went on in the "black hole" between the apostolic era and the appearance of the first bishops with rather exalted ideas about their job description, it's about as good a system as we are likely to end up with. The kind of "constitutional episcopacy" within Anglicanism combines the authority of the office–the commissioned and appointed overseer of the flock of Christ–with the authority of the people–the holy community of the faithful, commissioned and anointed in baptism. This balance of power gives both a sense of common calling and purpose among the whole people of God, and a sense of personal allegiance to the bishop as our "father" (and already "mother" in some parts of the Anglican Communion) in the household of faith.

All this means that Anglicans tend to be rather ambivalent about their bishops, as they are about other authority figures in English society; we are all in favor of them for as long as they leave us in peace and tell us what we want to hear.

There is an innate respect for the office of bishop, and a visit from the bishop is still an event that church members will turn out for. The bishop tends to be highly popular with the faithful as a symbol of our shared life and as a source of affirmation and good cheer in good times and bad. We tend to take much less notice of the bishop when he says something we don't agree with, and the days of bishops as public mediators, addressing crowds of workers in industrial disputes (a fairly common occurrence within living memory) have gone, along with gaiters and frock coats. Even within the household of faith, their authority has been so eroded by the many checks and balances at every stage of decision-making, that the bishop is no longer master of his own house. Perhaps the bishops had no choice, or didn't see it coming, but the end result is that they have sold their birthright for a mess of consultations, to the great detriment of the Church's mission.

Authority at the national level therefore lies with the synod or convention rather than the bishops, and it is perhaps only at the local level that a large degree of authority is vested in one person, the parish priest.

Although the parish priest's powers have not been untouched by the creeping paralysis of continual consultation, he or she remains on the whole a pope in his or her own parish. This should not for a moment be confused with unchallenged respect and adulation, both the English and the Americans having tamed their "holy man" long ago, allotting him a place in society equivalent to that of an ecclesiastical butler, a man not expected to hold opinions, but to conduct the ceremonies of the meal as they have always been conducted. In the last analysis people feel he is there to do what he is told.

So when it comes to authority, we Anglicans like to have our cake and eat it; we like the notion of an authority figure, but like to hedge him or her about with enough restrictions to ensure that, in the last resort, we can do our own thing. But of course politely, and with due deference, and after consultation.

12 Loitering with Intent
The Anglican Approach to Membership

St. Paul probably has quite a difficult time with Anglicans. Hot-headed impatient types like Paul (and like me for that matter) would prefer everything to be cut and dried, to know who's in and who's out, to know who our friends are. Such a certainty just isn't possible in the Anglican ethos. At times this drives me mad, at other times I can see (damn it!) that it is the only way for the followers of Jesus to behave.

Anglicanism has a big heart, and while this may yet prove to be its downfall, let's give it the benefit of the doubt and say that our dear old mum has wide open arms and a voluminous cozy bosom. She's always lovely to come home to, because the kettle's always on, and she never starts off with an interrogation as to where on earth we've been for the last ten years. It's love first, questions later. All this makes for a very untidy house, dirty washing everywhere and suitcases always in the hall, for there's always someone coming or going in this free and easy environment, and people loitering with good intent.

The definition of church membership is inevitably broad and hazy; it all depends on where you're starting out from, on where you start peeling the onion.

On the outer extremity we have (in England) all those who will enter "C of E" on their hospital admission form—still the majority of the adult population. They would see membership of the Church as an automatic right bestowed on them by their nationality, a membership that doesn't need thinking about because it is part and parcel of their Englishness. The Church colludes with this view by granting the privileges of membership on the sole basis of residency within a particular parish; baptism is usually available on demand, as are wedding ceremonies (albeit within a stricter legal framework) and funeral services. Even in the United States, with its complete separation of church and state, much importance is attached to the "Episcopal" label, and much trading on it by long-lapsed members eager to organize a wedding in a quaint church building with a suitably long aisle.

Although many priests make an attempt to invest these ceremonies with deeper meaning by requiring some indication of personal belief and commitment, they are usually worn down by the sense of outrage encountered among the public, and in the local press, for whom religion becomes the stuff of front page headlines once it can be rewritten as Bad News.

The typical Anglican line on this is that these rites of passage for an increasingly de-Christianized population are invaluable pastoral opportunities to be seized upon by a grateful Church. Those charged with the actual job of making a spiritual encounter out of a social event, where superstition rather than theology is likely to call the tune, may be pardoned for thinking otherwise.

As you may have gathered by now, I am all for a little more rigor in the catechumenate, but even I have to stop and wonder if in this whole question of membership we have been barking up the wrong tree, or straining at gnats to swallow camels (yes, a nice mixed metaphor there, but a camel up a tree is worth hanging on to. . .). By this I mean that whereas Jesus appears to have practically nothing to say about baptism, he has a very great deal to say about eating and drinking. His most significant and provocative prophetic act, repeated again and again, was to eat with "publicans and sinners," with the riff-raff, the outcasts, the untouchables. In so doing, he was attempting to make real and tangible the unconditional love of God for all his children; admission was no longer to be by ticket only.

In other words, Anglicans tend to get terribly excited about the membership question *precisely* at the wrong moment. Liturgically, this moment is symbolized in the Eucharist by that awful ceremonial shutting of the gates in the altar rail, with that final, irrevocable *click* by which we know we are expelled from the Garden, excluded forever from the holy of holies.

There are, of course, by now an increasing number of liturgical spaces (even Anglican ones) in which there is not an altar rail, or even an altar step, to be seen. Instead the table, and the feast prepared upon it, has been restored to the people, and stands in their midst, open and touchable, to remind us of our birthright as children of God. The Episcopal cathedral in Philadelphia is one such place, as is Portsmouth Cathedral in England, as is the renowned pioneer parish of St. Gregory of Nyssa in San Francisco.

St. Gregory's (see chapter four) has led the way in giving concrete expression to this radical insight of Jesus, challenging the Christian Church to think again about where it has its sticking points. The community of faith at St. Gregory's has reversed the usual liturgical order in the design of its new church building, so that the first thing the visitor comes across is the table set ready for a party, a powerful symbol of that unconditional love that welcomes us all with open arms. The Christian community first says "Come and eat, come and celebrate," and only after the Eucharist—and after the lunch served at the same table—is the route to the font discovered, a route that takes us out of the building into an enclosed garden where the waters of rebirth bubble in the baptistry set into the hillside.

First welcome: unconditional love expressed in an open table where no questions are asked; and only later initiation: tears of repentance and the costly business of surrender to God and reconciliation with those we have hurt.

Such a reversal of the customary pattern involves us in reversing also our usual priorities, tearing up the rule-book in relation to sharing the Eucharist, but rewriting the rules, and making them a lot tougher when it comes to enlisting new recruits in life-long service. Perhaps the early Church got us off on the wrong foot all those centuries ago when it locked the doors and banished the catechumens before breaking bread in the Eucharistic meal. It was perfectly understandable, but led us inevitably away from the practice of Jesus himself into the dark ages of restricted access and fenced altars, from which we are only just emerging.

Of course, one swallow doesn't a summer make, and one parish in San Francisco doesn't change the traditional emphasis on baptism and confirmation as the gateway to communion, and yet it is entirely appropriate that an Anglican parish should lead the way in asking the penetrating questions, challenging mainstream churches to think again. Amongst the churches of the Catholic tradition, only in the Anglican Communion could such freedom of expression exist, enabling a parish to explore and reinterpret and revitalize the ancient faith.

Anglicans are also free to set a little less store by the credal formulae beloved of previous Christian generations as tests of orthodox belief and qualification for membership of the Church. Although this makes us easy targets for modern-day pharisees always on the look-out for doctrinal indiscretions, many Christians would admit (even if some of them have to face away from the camera to do so) that when they recite the creed every Sunday they are repeating parrot-fashion a string of doctrinal statements which may no longer make any sense to them.[1] This is hardly surprising when we recall that creeds were first designed to defend the infant Christian Church against beliefs which were at that stage considered heretical. The contents of the creeds and their precise (often technical) phraseology represent carefully worked out responses to the controversies of the second and third centuries, when groups with opposing understandings of who Jesus was were wrestling for control of the Church.

This doesn't mean to say that we should cease to say the creeds, for they are a test of Church membership going back eighteen centuries, and they recall us to our common Christian heritage.[2] What we can and should do, however, is to look at them again in their historical context, unpack what the Church at that time was trying to say, and translate that message into the language and thought-forms of today.

108

The parish of St. Thomas, Indianapolis (Roman Catholic this time, but then progressive U.S. Catholics are honorary Anglicans anyway!) has done just that in a predominantly black neighborhood church. The community of faith in that place has wrestled with the problem of what the creed means for *them*, so that on entering its worship area you can pick up and reflect on this midwestern late twentieth-century version of what was first hammered out in the fourth-century Middle East. It begins:

> We believe in God, the eternal source and spirit of
> life, whom Jesus knew as father, and whom we call
> our loving parent, and to whose deeds we testify.

That version might not be exactly our cup of tea, but that hardly matters; the *process* is the thing—the wrestling with ideas and words in order to glimpse God more clearly and to be better able to communicate our faith to others.

In this regard the American Church is the very model of orthodoxy (whatever the African bishops say about us!), allowing neither jot nor tittle by way of deviation from the latest word from Nicea. Here America lags far behind England, where for many years the Church's official supplementary texts have encouraged the use of alternative affirmations of faith, now enshrined in *Common Worship*.

Membership for Anglicans is therefore more about incorporation into a community than conformity to a set of credal formulae or observance of a set of rules. I long ago gave up trying to provide baptism and marriage preparation classes, having come to realize that a period of participation in Sunday worship achieved more than a hundred classes divorced from liturgical formation. Christianity is caught not taught; unless we can catch a vision of how good it is simply to be around the altar of God with his people, then no amount of instruction will convince us otherwise. Conversely, once we have caught the vision, seen the point, then filling in the gaps of our knowledge is plain sailing. The head can always catch up with the heart, but the reverse process takes a lot longer, and for many individuals may never happen at all.

In these days of an increasingly post-Christian culture, potential members appear on the threshold coming from all kinds of backgrounds and experiences. The traditional pattern of infant baptism followed by confirmation in one's teens is losing ground as fewer people are baptized in infancy and there is a greater desire for full commitment in adulthood. The growth of the catechumenate movement is a healthy sign, as is the renewed emphasis on the Great Vigil of Easter as the time for initiation and renewal of commitment.

What membership actually entails will vary from parish to parish, but the basic norm is faithful Sunday worship, plus an evening per week when we can get to grips with the Christian life in greater depth. The big Sunday assembly and the small home meeting are both necessary for a healthy diet, for they feed and inform each other in the process of Christian formation. There can be no compulsion in a community of volunteers, but we can only build churches with building blocks that are on site, not those that are at home "having guests to stay" or away "down the Shore." In the final analysis the core membership is defined not by the parish priest but by self-selection as individuals opt in or opt out of what's on offer.

The Anglican approach to membership is that, while no one is going to compel you to do anything, we aim to create the kind of local Christian community in which you will want to do more, because you are known and valued, and your gifts recognized. Once you have decided to jump in with both feet, you have real scope for effective Christian service and for influencing the Church's way ahead. The possibilities are endless in a Church which has open access to (almost all!) its corridors of power.

Animal-lovers we may be, but nevertheless we recognize the limitations of the parrot as a model of the thinking, praying and practicing Christian. We love joining things, and we want others to join us in this great adventure of life together in the Church, but in our easy-going, and self-effacing and low-key way we would nevertheless want membership to *mean* something, and to move us further forward in a "journey of continual discovery," our horizons constantly changing as we go.[3]

At the end of the day, however, there is a growing hunch that joining an institution is not what it is all about, and that's why we should not take all the rules and regulation *too* seriously. The Church is absolutely essential, not as divinely appointed institution but as *a place to be*. And the place is not a building, but the assembly of faith, gathered every Sunday, where you hang out with Jesus and his crowd, catching onto ideas and visions which are liable to get you into trouble.

This makes everything a lot less neat and tidy, and most of our certainties get shaken up in the process, but you know how it is with Jesus: When you think you are in, you are out, and when you think you've blown it, you are invited to sit next to him at the party. But that's not such a bad picture of the Kingdom of God.

13 Seeing Both Sides
The Anglican Approach
to Moral Questions

"On the one hand ... but on the other" is the classical caricature of an Anglican trying to come to a decision on a moral question. The Anglican position is easily dismissed as nothing more than a total inability to come down off the fence. All too conscious of this, we tend to write ourselves off as moral theologians, apologizing for our own woolly-mindedness. In fact it is when we grapple with moral problems, feeling very uncertain of the unequivocal rights and wrongs of the matter, that Anglicans discover (again by accident and much to our surprise) that we have the most to offer a perplexed world, and can hold our heads high within the community of Christian churches.

Certainly we see no virtue in weakness and prevarication; we want to be firm and clear in our advice to those who seek the "Christian" way in a violently troubled world in which society is disintegrating in the face of rampant individualism. But it is becoming increasingly difficult to discern what is in fact truly "Christian."

To arrive at what is an authentic Christian response to any contemporary issue, we are for the most part best-guessing what Jesus of Nazareth would have done had he been here now. This is exceptionally difficult for the simple reason that it is highly likely that the concept of an organization of his followers existing two thousand years hence would have astonished the Gospel writers, for they expected Christ to return at any moment. His recorded words are almost entirely devoid of detailed instructions on what to do, where and when. Equally, Jesus himself is concerned chiefly with attitudes and relationships, rather than precise codes of conduct, and we shall look in vain in the Gospels for detailed guidance on what to do in response to the moral dilemmas of today, many of which are thrown up by humankind's ceaseless advance in knowledge and technical ability, whether genetic engineering or nuclear physics.

Occasionally we come across fixed points, such as the prohibition against the taking of human life, which are constants for us as much as for the first-century Palestinian crowd that listened to Jesus on this subject, and who later were able to observe what he himself did when his theory was tested in practice. Even here, however, the Church has been busy muddying the waters over the centuries, dreaming up all kinds of exclusion clauses such as the development of the doctrine of the so-called just war, or the concept of the State having the right to impose the death penalty in certain circumstances.

For the most part, then, we are indeed lost in a moral maze, and Anglicans, being familiar with the Hampton Court Maze incident in Jerome K. Jerome's *Three Men in a Boat*, are instinctively dubious of people like Harris who assert that "It's very simple. It's absurd to call it a maze . . . we'll just walk round for ten minutes, and then go and get some lunch."[1] Anglicans find absolute certainty on moral questions an elusive goal, and for very good reasons which take us to the heart of the Anglican psyche.

To begin with, Anglicans are basically nice. We start out resolutely enough, with a very real desire to give a lead, to hold the line, and not to appear wimpish, but are bedeviled (or "begoddled") by a very English sense of fair play coupled with a conviction that Jesus' distinctive characteristic was compassion rather than judgment. Our wonder at the grace of God is exceeded only by our awareness of human frailty, and we are haunted by the words of good Mr. John Bradford (1510–55), no doubt the first moral theologian of the Anglican school, who exclaimed, upon seeing some criminals on their way to execution, "But for the grace of God there goes John Bradford."[2]

We tend only too easily to be moved by the exceptional case and are as a result poor lawmakers. Whenever we are on the point of preaching a fierce sermon or enforcing a cast-iron rule, we seem always to be reminded of a particular story of an individual who has broken the rules but has been blessed by God. Perhaps King David, but more likely me. And so we mount the pulpit or wield the pen with slightly less certainty than we would like, being all-too-conscious of the possibility of preaching to others only to find ourselves disqualified.[3]

Secondly, total self-confidence in these matters can flourish only in a climate of intellectual totalitarianism in one form or another—theological positions with which Anglicans find themselves deeply uneasy. Absolute moral certainty demands cast-iron dogma in which there is no room for debate or uncertainty. Such an approach requires blind, unquestioning obedience to one of two forms of fundamentalism: belief in the literal truth of Holy Scripture as faxed through from God's administration HQ, or belief in an ecclesiastical structure to which the Holy Spirit has handed over sole trading rights. In other words, to believe that the exit from the moral maze is always immediately to hand, or at least just around the next corner, one has to be deluded and as daft as Harris.

The Anglican approach to moral questions is built on the three pillars of Scripture, tradition and common sense: on what the New Testament says, on what the Christian consensus has always tended to be, and on what works and rings true to our own day-by-day experience of God's activity in creation. None of these three is held to be sacrosanct to the exclusion of the other two, but they inform and enrich one another as the Church journeys slowly toward a deeper understanding of the wisdom of God.

It is for this reason that Anglicans find it difficult to jump to attention every time the bishops issue a statement or produce a report on an aspect of Christian ethics, because our instinct is to check out their findings both with the New Testament and with our own experience of how things work in the real world.

Likewise, we are not ones for rattling off chapter and verse of biblical texts taken in isolation, because we know that we must first discover in what sense those texts have been understood and applied by succeeding generations of Christians and in particular by those who have oversight of the Church today.

Amazingly, these checks and balances have led to a *modus operandi* which is far more robust than is generally realized, and which under closer scrutiny bears up well beside the rhetoric of others. Although the popular notion is that the Anglican Church is a bit of a pushover when upholding moral principles, the reality is otherwise.

Take, for example, marriage discipline. For far longer than any other mainstream Christian church in England, the Church of England has held the line on remarriage after divorce, continuing to uphold the principle of a life-long obligation, and considering it inappropriate for the marriage service in church to be made available when one of the parties has a previous partner still living. Its regulations were relaxed only in 2002.

For all its faults, Anglican practice in England has compared favorably with that of other traditions. In the Free Churches, church weddings after divorce seem to be available on demand, while in the Roman Church the question is circumnavigated through the contrivance of annulment (80,000 of which are granted annually worldwide) and through the device of not counting the previous marriage of a non-Catholic partner. In these ways, participants are helped, not to admit their mistakes and begin again, but to proceed as if their first marriage was a figment of their theological imagination. For divorced Roman Catholics seeking remarriage in church, and whose first wedding was conducted in another Christian tradition, the procedure is even simpler, as the first marriage doesn't even appear on the canon lawyer's radar screen. The Anglican finds such stratagems distasteful because they are more concerned with legality than reality, and are at base simply dishonest. We put a high premium on honesty, even if this results in a fair bit of dirty laundry being washed in public. That is a small price to pay for freedom from double-think.

Of more critical importance on today's overcrowded planet is the subject of birth control, and here the Anglican approach has always been to resist any suggestion that procreation is the sole purpose of sexual love within marriage. We have Cranmer to thank for this, who, in his first Prayer Book of 1549, brought about "revolutionary liturgical change by asserting that marriage could be fun."[4] Developments in medical knowledge which make available a number of methods of contraception should benefit all humankind, and be used as widely as possible to decrease the birth rate, especially in Third World countries racked by poverty. To dream up theological reasons for frustrating the widest possible application of this knowledge, and restricting birth control to one method among many, appears to the Anglican mind as perverse in the extreme.

Homosexuality is the current hot potato in the field of Christian ethics, one in which tensions have opened up within the Anglican Communion on a north-south divide. As scientific understanding of sexual orientation has grown (it's not something you choose, it's something you are), bishops in America and England are becoming increasingly reluctant to perpetuate regulations that discriminate on the basis of a person's genetic makeup. In fact, the vast majority of bishops have been ordaining gay people for years, it's just that they haven't thought about it or faced it as a question of intent. This has given a handful of bishops from the southern hemisphere a field day. Apparently having no work to do in their own dioceses, they have taken to wandering through the United States, denouncing any thinking bishop they can find, and confirming anything that moves.

Here again, the Anglican approach is to proceed with caution, refusing to bow to pressure from either gay activists or right-wing fundamentalists. Somewhere in the middle will be found the way of sanctified common sense, in which reality can be recognized, good affirmed and wrongdoing condemned. It will probably be found that the real question for our society is not sexual orientation, but the development of the God-given capacity for life-long faithfulness and sacrificial love.

To make such values common currency in every culture, we shall need to develop what Hans Küng calls a "global ethic," in which all the great religions underpin a shared understanding of, and upholding of, those human qualities and characteristics that make for a just, free and mutually accepting society. To become common property, the highest and truest values of civilization will need to be freed from claims of ownership by any one religious tradition. No one faith has a monopoly on goodness.

Anglicans have resigned themselves to not doing very well in the ethics paper (when I was ordained it wasn't even on the syllabus). We are well aware that the fastest-growing ecclesiastical communities are those offering cast-iron certainties in theology and ethics, an all-in package holiday away from thought and struggle, which is extremely attractive to a harassed society. Bishop John Saxby puts it brilliantly when he suggests that Anglicans in their better moments prefer staircases to lifts (elevators), because we want to be involved and engaged in life, not whizzing unmindfully through it cocooned in our own safe little world.[5]

We know however, that life isn't like that. There are no neat solutions packed away between two covers, whether in the New Testament, the New Catechism, or Chairman Mao's Little Red Book. If ever Anglicans allow themselves a less-than-totally-humble thought, it is that one day the others will stop playing games and come and join us in the muddy waters. As Anglicans, our experience is that the stepping stones that will get us across are hidden and slippery, not obvious and bone dry and clear of the water, and the only way to find them is by getting wet. On the whole, we prefer that to starting out dry-shod and falling in halfway; the shock can kill you.

14 Sending Us Out
The Anglican Approach to the Wider Community

Here's where the Anglican feels on safer territory. Indeed for many Anglicans, the wider community is always *us* rather than *them*, such is the strength of our conviction that the Church, like Jesus, must lay down its life (and its boundaries) for the sake of those to whom it is sent as a messenger of good news.

This all-inclusive approach is especially true of England, for historical reasons; Anglicans in the U.S. need to work on this a little more if they are to shake themselves free of denominationalism (a deeply un-Anglican notion). The proposition that, for example, an Episcopal diocese should not open up a new mission in an area short of registered Episcopalians should be anathema to a church with even an ounce of apostolic zeal, let alone one with the energy of Cuthbert, Boniface, Thomas Bray, Frank Weston, Jackson Kemper, or David Pendleton Oakhater in its bloodstream.

Typically, we like to be out and about getting things done, not least because we are easily embarrassed when God starts getting personal, or his servants emotional. Like the kindly neighbor in the house of the newly bereaved, we may not know what to *say*, but we always seem to know what to *do*; we make a cup of tea.

The Church of England's sense of commission to every single individual resident within our national boundaries brings with it a keen sense of responsibility for those who, in whatever sense, are our neighbors. This makes us uneasy about the drawing of boundaries and the over-exact definition of who are "in" and who are "out." Anglicans tend to set out their stall, throw open their doors, and encourage all to feel they have a right to enter. Any exclusion is entirely self-imposed by those who choose to go elsewhere, like those followers of Jesus who, on hearing what he had to say, "no longer went about with him" (John 6:66).

Central to this open-house policy is the realization of just how widely and unconditionally Jesus himself defined *neighbor*; and as a result we cannot bring ourselves to pass by on the other side. If this at times makes us look as if we are poking our collective nose into other people's business, then so be it. Better to do something (even if we get it wrong) than to stand idly by.

The Church's relationship to the wider community—how that community is identified and celebrated and entered into dialogue with—is an important question to address in whatever kind of situation the Church finds itself.

At the national level, the Church of England is like a department store with a very large doorway, in which we can window-gaze at things we like but don't want to buy, shelter from the rain when a sudden storm comes, or even spend the night if we're down on our luck. The day we put a metal grille over the shop front is the day we close down altogether, for the role of the Church is to be "there" for everyone, and to rise to the occasion when called upon to do so.

At the local level, things will be a little more moribund. Although the historic English designation of the priest as *parson* is not a favorite of mine (it smacks of a world when a tame priest was kept hanging around the place to provide services as and when required), it does at least recall us to the role of the priest as the representative *person* of the local community. It is for this reason that you will find many a parish priest accepting all kinds of roles in the wider community—chair of school governors, committee member of an interest group or sports club, even elected representative in local government—as part of a deliberate policy to weave together ever more effectively the overlapping communities of church and parish.

This ideal is perhaps more recognizable and realizable in stable and mainly prosperous communities in a rural or suburban setting, where the Church is working away to patch and strengthen the fabric of local society. It becomes more fraught when we come to those areas of severe social deprivation in our cities where the parish priest can easily become a one-person social services department if so inclined. It is in these areas, where need is most conspicuous, that the Church's approach to the wider community is in sharpest focus.

The headlong rush of the Episcopal Church into commuter ministry is to be regretted. Having spent thirty-four years as a parish priest in England living "over the shop," it was a culture shock to find myself in the United States living six miles from the physical center of my ministry. Delightful though it is in many ways to live at some distance from the desk and the altar (I love my morning train!), I don't kid myself that this is other than theologically and pastorally indefensible.

"I'm not called to be a social worker" is an understandable riposte on the part of many priests concerned at the dilution of the distinctively Christian message in the midst of the Church's developing role as general "provider." This inner conflict is felt especially in urban areas of deprivation where, in our "benefits culture," clergy and church workers are faced with demands for bus fares or baby food rather than Bibles. This chorus of practical need reaches its crescendo around five o'clock on a Friday evening as the social security offices close, the long weekend stretches ahead, and yarns are spun about checks failing to arrive and relatives ill in distant hospitals.

Getting the balance right is a tricky business, and we've often got it wrong, either locking ourselves into a spiritual ivory tower, or exhausting our limited human and financial resources in community work that may improve circumstances (for a while) but doesn't change people. Anglicans can, however, take heart from a long history of work with the wider community in which solid achievement has borne fruit that lasts. Education is a good example of where the Church in previous centuries led the way in pioneering the provision of facilities which we now take for granted as part of the fabric of society, and of the State's basic provision for its citizens.

In England, the National Society, founded by Joshua Watson in 1811, strove to establish a system of elementary education across the country, with training colleges to train the teachers for the new schools (the first college opened in 1841). The Church led the way and the State followed, but took a little time to catch up, not establishing its first Board Schools until 1870. Gradually the State came to play an increasing part in the financial support of the Church schools, so that today both Church and State schools shelter beneath the same Local Education Authority umbrella, albeit with differing legal frameworks enshrining different educational philosophies. Although the State's educational umbrella now offers shelter to every child in the country, it is interesting to note that it is the church schools within the local education authority system which are top of the pops. They can usually boast waiting lists because they have established a reputation for good teaching and, even more significant in a disintegrating and directionless society, for the provision of a moral framework for young people to steer by.

In the days long ago, before training conferences were invented to keep the clergy off the streets, their favorite occupation was to form themselves into little groups and societies of like-minded thinkers in order to translate theory into action and generally make the world a better place. It seems the late eighteenth and early nineteenth centuries abounded in such intellectual pressure groups—the Clapham Sect (of Evangelicals) and the corresponding Hackney Phalanx (or Clapton Sect) of High Churchmen—and they were not talking shop, but were engines for social change arising from theological conviction.

The Clapham Sect could boast of William Wilberforce, crusader for the abolition of the slave trade, as a luminary, while the Hackney Phalanx had Joshua Watson, founder of the National Society, as a paid-up leading member. It is significant that Wilberforce was dissuaded by his guru John "How Sweet the Name of Jesus Sounds" Newton from seeking ordination, on the grounds that his great oratorical gifts could advance the Christian cause more effectively in Parliament (of which he was already a member) than in the pulpit. This vocation of Christian service to society has become a well-trodden path in Anglican tradition.

This large-scale vision can be seen transposed into a minor key by priests who, during the nineteenth and early twentieth centuries, labored in the stoniest corners of the English vineyard. Fired up usually by one of the several religious revivals which freshened up the Church during this period, they strode into action clutching Bible or crucifix in one hand and soup bowl in the other. These were the "slum priests" who took on the toughest jobs available, ministering to those living in abject poverty in the burgeoning cities of Victorian England.

These initiatives were given an intellectual coherence by the Christian Socialist Movement which, founded during the "Hungry Forties" of the nineteenth century, sought to bring about social reform. It was backed by theologians of the stature of F. D. Maurice, whose determination to apply Christian principles to the real world cost him his job as Professor of Theology at King's College, London. Although the movement lost momentum as an educative and political force, its long-term fruits were seen in the formation of trade unions and the early co-operative societies, and even today can be discerned at work leavening the lump of New Labour's massive 1997 election majority.[1]

Ever since, this dogged tradition of incarnational involvement in the struggles of humankind has refused to lie down and die, and has served constantly to prick the bubble of the Church's self-importance and preoccupation with the sacred understood in isolation from the secular. It is glimpsed during the First World War in the person of Geoffrey Studdert Kennedy, priest-poet, and the War's most illustrious chaplain, known to the troops as "Woodbine Willie" because of the cigarettes he liberally distributed. His fierce compassion for the men thrown to needless deaths, and his ability to put into everyday language the eternal mysteries of God, life, and death, make him a giant among the men of God.[2]

On the other side of the Atlantic we find that this instinctive Anglican approach has borne much fruit. The Episcopal Church's finest hour came in the Civil Rights era of the 1960s and 70s, when its insistence on the priority of justice in a society riven by incredible racial prejudice and violence won it an honored place among the liberators and (as proof of this) lost it many of its members at the same time. Today, major metropolitan dioceses have community service departments with payrolls of many hundreds "making a difference" for countless numbers of the disadvantaged in a country with no social security net to catch the casualties of urban life.

This instinct for social action has never died, although it sometimes takes a catastrophe or two to shake the Church out of its complacency, to dust itself down and once again to wake up to the realities of life. Civil unrest in the most deprived areas of English cities in the 1980s (chiefly South London and Liverpool) jolted the Church into action, and following publication in 1985 of *Faith in the City* (the report of the Archbishop of Canterbury's Commission on Urban Priority Areas) the Church Urban Fund was born. This Fund achieved not merely the distribution of £18 million in starter grants to church-led projects for social action in our inner cities, momentous though that was, but the re-education of the whole Church to think in terms of social action.

In particular, the Church of England was shown how its great asset of a "corner shop" in every town and village could at last be brought fully into play. This building's "burden" was revealed as a potential boon, and countless church premises in key locations of need were transformed into thriving centers of worship, training and community service. This process is not restricted to urban areas, for the countryside has deprivation of a different kind, in which village facilities are continually forced to close in the face of the car-borne rush to the nearest town. Anyone without a car is left stranded, like a whale on the beach when the tide goes out. In situations of need in rural areas, the parish church is beginning to rediscover its medieval role as a covered gathering space for the whole community. Examples are springing up all over the place of church buildings in which the nave is cleared of pews (that's real sacrifice for you!) and re-equipped as a social facility for the whole village, while the chancel becomes a worship space appropriate for present-day needs.

Salvation does not, of course, come through soup kitchens or seniors' luncheon clubs, and half the clients at the drop-in center may be taking the Church for a ride, but then so may half the "respectable" people who read lessons and sit on church councils. We're all into cheating on God in one way or another, and putting yourself on the line for others is a risky business, as Jesus of Nazareth found. In the prayer at the end of the Eucharist, however, we offer God "our souls and bodies to be made a living sacrifice," and the current malaise at all levels of society provides us with an opportunity to make our word our bond. In having compassion for the crowds "because they were harassed and helpless"[3] the Church finds its own soul. Neither Wilberforce nor Woodbine Willie, Absalom Jones nor Julia Chester Emery need spin in their graves, for their message did not go unheeded. Our earnest desire as Anglicans still is to be numbered among those who "hear the word of God and put it into practice."[4]

15 Taking a Lower Seat
The Anglican Approach to Other Traditions and Faiths

Here is Anglicanism at its most Anglican, and here it is in transition. By instinct Anglicans tend to think well of others and modestly of themselves, and at the same time they find themselves caught up in a global realignment of believers and seekers after truth.

In this global realignment, labels are becoming secondary to the reality of the encounter with that-we-call-God. This is the life force revealed to Moses as I AM WHO I AM, or even more simply as I AM—the mystery of existence personified and initiating a relationship with us (Exod. 3:14).

When we come face to face with the stupendous truth that the mind behind the 100,000 million stars of our galaxy, the human body or a single snowflake actually wants to get to know us and spend time with us, the anxious questions, "Are you saved?" or "Are you a Catholic?" or "Do you keep the Deobandi Islamic code?" are enquiries of monumental inconsequence. The pursuit of exclusive religious purity has bedeviled humankind from day one and is coming to be seen as a fruitless obsession indicative of a concept of God that is basically too small to fit.

But we rush on too fast. Before examining the Anglican contribution to the part played by Christianity on the world stage among the major religions, we need to take a look at Anglicans in their relations with other Christians, that is, with other traditions within the one Christian fold (which are not other *religions,* as is so often asserted).

For Anglicans, by far the most important issue in ecumenical relations is the reunion of the Western Church—the reintegration of Canterbury with Rome. The bitter divisions of the sixteenth century are not our battles, and in many remarkable ways both communions have come full circle, making nonsense of our former exclusive categories and precise distinctions.

Go to the United States, for example, to discover how the Roman Catholic Church, in its remarkable expansion program into the suburbs of the great cities, is designing worship spaces which in their layout and design proclaim the primitive Christian (and thereby Reformation) principles of the community of the baptized celebrating together word and sacrament. In a complementary movement of the Spirit, liturgical renewal in England has already brought about a situation where the Anglican celebration of the eucharistic rite proclaims both continuity with the primitive church and common cause with the rest of the Western Church. In our cathedrals, votive candles are lit, shrines of the saints visited and confessions heard; history has overtaken us, and the Spirit has made fun of our previous obsessions with what is "High" and what is "Low."

What we in England have to remember is that relations between Canterbury and Rome have been bedeviled by history. In no other country in the world are there two claimants to the ancient title, two hierarchies claiming to provide authentic apostolic authority, two Catholic churches. No wonder that relations have been strained, and that claim and counter-claim, accusation and heated denial, have colored our dialogue until now. In terms of the denouncements of old, the Roman is for the Anglican a "recent" foreign interloper (a Papist), while the Anglican is for the Roman a member of a state-controlled Protestant sect.

Against this background of mutual insults it was imperative that when official top-level conversations between the two communions were inaugurated, both sides should escape the English trap. Accordingly, following the visit of Archbishop Michael Ramsey to Pope Paul VI in Rome in 1966, their Common Declaration initiated the setting up of an Anglican-Roman Catholic Commission which was thoroughly international on both sides. Under the joint chairmanship of a senior bishop from each communion, and meeting over the last thirty years in venues across the world, the Commission has made startling progress. To read the reports of the Commission so far published is to roll back the pages of history, rediscovering common ground in primitive Christianity and redefining former causes of division in ways that could unite us. The Commission's work is so heartening that one wonders what all the fuss had been about, as we proudly clung to our differences down the centuries.

This détente was further strengthened by the gracious and generous gesture by Pope John Paul II, during his visit to England in 1982, in kneeling in prayer alongside Archbishop Robert Runcie in Canterbury Cathedral and acknowledging his brother bishop as the successor of Augustine, first Archbishop of Canterbury.

Sad to say, all this good work was almost undone in the early 1990s, when a couple of big wrenches were thrown into the works which until then were humming along quite nicely (but we threw in one each, to retain a proper sense of balance). First the Vatican, after keeping us all waiting for an incredibly long time, in 1993 finally gave the Commission's findings an extremely lukewarm (well, freezing) response, and then later that same year the General Synod's vote to admit women to the priesthood provided another serious setback. Thankfully, the Commission appears to remain unbowed and continues its good work.

At the Protestant end of the bridge, talks in England on reunion with the Methodist Church (hewn from the Anglican rock two centuries ago) continue, having foundered in 1969 and again in 1972; while the Poorvoo Statement, ratified by General Synod in 1996, took us much closer to the Nordic and Baltic Lutheran Churches.

In the United States, 2002 saw the inauguration of the visionary *Call to Common Mission* (*CCM*) between the Episcopal

Church and the Evangelical Lutheran Church of America, which authorizes full interchangeability of ministries and from which it is hoped full union will inevitably flow in due course. *CCM* must also make God smile, as Lutherans, nervous of episcopacy, discover that Episcopal bishops have all the trappings but little power, and that their Lutheran counterparts have long been practicing effective episcopal authority without realizing it. There is a loosening up at last.

Meanwhile, back at the ranch, ecumenical progress at grassroots level continues at a leisurely pace. Here the thing to remember is that until the nineteenth century, Anglicans in an English context saw themselves quite simply as *the* Church. All other Christian groups (including Roman Catholics) were, again quite simply, *Non-conformists* in that they chose not to conform to the practices of the English Church but to opt out and do their own thing. Because Church and society were seen as one, to opt out of the Church was equivalent to committing social hara-kiri. Even after the danger of physical persecution had passed, Christians of other traditions continued to experience no little inconvenience. Non-conformists were barred from holding office under the Crown until 1829, and from university entrance until 1871.

If Anglicans don't come out of this smelling sweetly, it should be remembered that such restrictive legislation had arisen in a period of intense religious feeling when blood had been shed on account of the finer points of Christian doctrine, and when doctrinal non-conformity was synonymous in the popular mind with disloyalty to the national cause. Furthermore, the proportion of the population affected by these prohibitions was comparatively small. Since the removal of all discriminatory legislation from the statute books in the nineteenth century, Anglicans have leaned over backwards to make up for past misdeeds with a generosity of spirit which is not only typically English in its self-deprecating nature, but also symptomatic of a Church at ease with itself and its role in life.

For example, the removal in recent years of restrictions concerning participation in the Eucharist at Anglican altars, and in eligibility for election to parochial church councils, means that the Church of England has established a genuine open-house policy with regard both to worship and to participation in the life of the local church. As a result, the onus of non-participation is placed fairly and squarely on the individual. The Church offers a general invitation to the party, and only the scruples of those invited can cast a cloud over the proceedings.

Theologically, a member of the English Church is a Christian first and an Anglican second, and this is highly significant when it comes to relations with other Christian churches. The Anglican looks askance at members of other traditions who assert their brand label, rather than their Christian calling, as their primary distinguishing mark. We note with wry amusement, for example, that whereas the priest-poet R. S. Thomas (as an Anglican) is usually described as a Christian writer, Graham Greene was always referred to as a *Catholic* one, as though the Christian calling wasn't quite up to scratch. Admittedly a good deal of such nomenclature can be attributed to the media, who love building up mystique (and who, most ironically, regard Roman Catholics very much like ecclesiastical freemasons), but we recognize also that anxious labeling of this kind[1] can spring from an insecurity inappropriate to today's increasingly relaxed atmosphere.

In the face of the obsessive-labeling syndrome, the ecumenical scene has need of someone in a baggy suit, the easy-going bumbler of the common room who, feeling he has nothing to lose, will be sufficiently at ease with himself to take the lead. This is the vocation of the Anglican Communion, in working for more effective ecumenical co-operation between different Christian traditions in the same locality. Because ecclesiastical one-upmanship is not our cup of tea, the political maneuvering of others often passes us by, and when we notice at all, we are amused rather than angry. In joint projects with ecumenical partners, Anglicans will tend to put seventy-five percent of the cash on the table and cheerfully allow the others seventy-five percent of the say, but that's the way we are. In the end we cannot quite bring ourselves to be any other way, stubbornly believing that there are very few ecclesiastical principles which are matters of life and death, the gospel setting other priorities before us.

So nowadays the Anglican household is accepted by many as a kind, old, easy-going auntie figure who has lots of people round to tea with no questions asked, who serves good cakes and has left a bit in her will to simply everyone. She's often taken for a ride by the rogues in the neighborhood, and spitefully mocked by the arrogant upstarts recently converted to the latest enthusiasm. But she smiles on through it all, winning our respect as well as our affection, the older we get. Because she's never pushy we all feel comfortable at going back to see her, no matter how long we've been away or how far we've traveled.

When it comes to relations with other faiths, the same gradual evolution from the primeval slime can be seen at work. When I was ordained, the definitive text on the question of Christianity and other religions was John 14:6, straight from the shoulder, both barrels: "No one comes to the Father except through me." Living in a North of England town with a Sikh neighbor on one side and a Muslim on the other, I found such unthinking triumphalism an embarrassment. The development in thought underlying this change in perception (in which I don't think I am alone) can be attributed largely to the fact that England, certainly as far as our major urban conurbations are concerned, is now a multi-cultural and multi-faith society.

Moving from mono-cultural Peterborough to multi-cultural Huddersfield required a theological shift as well as a removal van. The experience at Junior School of our then six-year-old daughter helped bring it home to us. Whereas in the post-Christian culture of Peterborough hardly anyone in her class believed in God, in her Huddersfield class (in which she was one of only four white faces) everyone did.

Living in a parish where the most active and vibrant community of faith is the local Sikh gurdwara, I was humbled again and again by the Christ-like people I came to know from the other great religious traditions, making parallel journeys to God. Like all religions (including Christianity) they have their nuts and their fanatics hiding behind religious slogans and ecclesiastical status, but if we concentrate on those genuine souls seeking God and seeking holiness, then they have as much to give as to learn. We may have found the supreme way and the most straightforward route, but there are still some useful short cuts to be discovered if only we have the humility to listen to other experienced travelers.

To take but one example, we can be very snooty about our unique experience of praying to God as *Dad* through Jesus our Lord, but perhaps it's time we grew up. Whereas the prayer of Islam, for instance, seems to be a paean of praise to God who is great and magnificent and holy, and an affirmation of obedience to his will, the prayer of Christianity seems all too often characterized by petition rather than praise. For all our intimacy with God, won for us by Jesus Christ, we can exhibit an immature dependency on God typical of a rights-and-benefits society disempowered by an over-protective welfare state.

The Christian track record on this front has been very shaky indeed, and Anglicans have contributed more than their six pennyworth to the cause of Christian imperialism on the world stage.

The long history of persecution of the Jews redounds to Christianity's eternal shame, and will no doubt prove to be one of the supreme ironies of human history—Jews being harassed and put to death by the alleged followers of the most famous Jew of all time. The nadir of the Christian story with regard to other faiths, however, must surely be the Crusades, in which, from the eleventh to the fifteenth centuries, an unholy alliance of the Church and the military attempted to wrest the Holy Places of Palestine from Islam. Amazingly, the very last attempt to use force in converting others to the cause of the Prince of Peace was not until 1543, when Henry VIII joined forces with the Emperor Charles V to mount an expedition to fight the Turks. This was mainly a political ploy to get at the French (with whom the Turks had formed an alliance), but nevertheless Cranmer was required to act as chief recruiting officer for this "holy" piece of thuggery.

The Crusades show just how easy it is to lose sight of the wood of the common search for God, through fixing attention on this particular Jewish or Muslim tree. They also reveal a Christian fixation with territorial space that has no support whatsoever from the recorded teachings of Jesus of Nazareth or from early Christian practice. It is astonishing to us today that such a saintly luminary as Bernard of Clairvaux, he of the lyrical sermons on the Song of Songs, should have exhorted Christians to throw themselves bloodthirstily on the infidels in the Second Crusade of 1147, and should have upbraided them, in their subsequent military failure, for their lack of *faith*! The "hideous carnage"[2] wreaked by the Crusaders in capturing Jerusalem in 1099 contrasts sharply with the honorable and merciful conduct of the Saracens when they took the city in 1187.

Today, with an Arab bishop in Jerusalem,[3] the Anglican Communion plays its part in reminding the world that Palestine has a considerable Christian population, and that lasting peace in the Middle East demands more than simplistic solutions from right-wing Christians who would equate current Israeli regimes with the biblical children of Israel. Jerusalem is *the* holy city of the world, and until it belongs to no one and to everyone, strife will continue.

In more recent centuries, Anglicans, in common with all Christian churches of the West, channeled this crusading zeal into overseas missionary work on a vast scale. Evangelicals and Catholics, each founding their own missionary societies,[4] vied with each other to excel in the work of exporting God the Englishman (or American) to the four corners of the globe. Tremendous, heroic work was done, and the booming churches of Africa are today a particularly fruitful harvest from that faithful and sacrificial sowing. At the same time, it was difficult if not impossible for missionaries from great colonial powers to separate spiritual from cultural evangelization in the days when enculturation of the gospel was a distant concept, glimpsed by only the far-sighted pioneer. With the Commandments and Communion came the Coca-Cola.

Friends were rightly envious when they learned that one third of our parish community in Huddersfield was Afro-Caribbean, but they mistakenly imagined that our worship would thereby be characterized by exuberance and lack of inhibition. They forget that those from the West Indies who worship with us now are the products of a long process of reverse-enculturation by the Anglican Church in distant lands, which, instead of retelling the Christian story in local dialect, required the locals to learn a new language of worship which was alien to them and through which their natural characteristics were suppressed. As a result, our brothers and sisters from the West Indies, for example, are burdened with dress codes and behavior patterns for worship, reminiscent of our own pre-war culture, that we ourselves have long discarded. In our own small way we have done a bit of a St. Bernard.

In the face of all that has gone before, the glorious, the good, and the missing of the mark, we can thank God today for prophets such as Hans Küng (another honorary Anglican) who recall us to a new beginning, in penitence and faith, alongside Jew and Muslim, with whom we share spiritual descent from Abraham. These three great monotheistic religions, sharing three interwoven revelations of the one true God, should together be the pathfinders of a new "alliance for God" in the face of the hedonistic materialism and democratic imperialism that are derailing the Western world. Even that fierce defender of the English Church, Dr. Samuel Johnson, was moved to remark, "as to religion, have we heard all that a disciple of Confucius, all that a Mahometan, can say for himself?"[5]

In the context of English cities, where so many church schools are multi-cultural, Anglicans could have a particular part to play in pioneering a new religious education syllabus expressing, not a watered-down Christian faith giving offense to no one, but a brave new religious education syllabus for all God-seekers. This would draw on the teachings of scriptures and prophets of each great religious tradition, to affirm and celebrate the common inheritance of faith shared by the three great monotheistic religions which can look to Abraham as their patriarch, and which together, but only together, might have something to offer a world polarized by the blind certainties of politics or religion.

Only a step of this magnitude would do justice to the critical situation we face when Western culture has for all intents and purposes forsaken God, and finds, on the occasions it turns to religion to ask for bread, merely the barren stone of religious confrontation, both between major faiths and within them. The warning of Jesus of Nazareth that only by their fruits will people of truth and peace and justice be recognized needs to ring in our ears a lot more loudly and incessantly. Anglicans, by virtue of our own history and characteristics, could do a lot to turn up the volume.

16 Where Do We Go From Here?

Becoming an Anglican is rather like crossing a frontier into a new country. This new country is not a foreign land, but rather our deepest selves recognized for the first time. To quote T. S. Eliot again:

> We shall not cease from exploration
> And the end of all our exploring
> Will be to arrive where we started
> And know the place for the first time.[1]

Although we will have to learn new things—a new language of worship and thought perhaps, new ways of seeing things and responding to events—the process is primarily a journey, and a journey inward. In his book *The Hero with a Thousand Faces*, Joseph Campbell draws together the themes common to all the great religious quests, across the world and throughout history, and clearly discerns the journey inward as an experience known to all seekers after truth:

> . . . we have only to follow the thread of the hero-path. And where we had thought to find an abomination, we shall find a god; where we had

thought to slay another, we shall slay ourselves;
where we had thought to travel outward, we shall
come to the centre of our existence; where we
had thought to be alone, we shall be with all
the world.[2]

In an English context, becoming an Anglican is inevitably bound
up with developing an instinctive approach to things which is
quintessentially English—those qualities that I have attempted to
identify in the previous chapters. In other parts of the world that
Englishness may be very muted, but it is there nevertheless,
enriching our striving to build local Christian communities that
are free, exploratory, dignified, joyous, and open (and of course
understated, and of course with a sense of humor).

You will find the immigration officials at the frontier into this
new country kindness itself. They will not glower at you as they
compare you with that ridiculous passport photograph, nor will
they interrogate you or try to catch you out, or demand that you
open your suitcase. On the whole we are fairly laid-back about
instruction courses—a few chats with the parish priest is sometimes all you will get—but we have no intention of being made to
feel inadequate on this score. We believe that Christian initiation
is ninety percent incorporation and ten percent indoctrination.
We know that we can offer *real* community, intimate and
demanding, where the Risen Lord is encountered, not just in the
breaking of bread, but in the coffee-hour and at the soup kitchen,
in the prayer-group and at the local hospital, in the neighborhood
clean-up or at the peace vigil. That's where we rest our case, at
the sharp point of the Christian life.

As you would expect, it's all very low-key, and free and easy.
Confirmation is a simple and straightforward ceremony which no
one need find daunting. It's best of course if you're an adult, so
that the event can be a real dedication of your whole self to God,
a kind of "lay ordination," a joyous confirmation of the "provisional booking" made on your behalf at your baptism as an infant.
The best of all possible times for doing the deed is of course the
Easter Vigil, imaginatively celebrated (preferably before dawn) to
recall the whole community to the Christian mystery of death and
rebirth, and if you're not already baptized, so much the better, as

then you may experience in one glorious go the whole shooting match of baptism, confirmation and first communion.

If you've already been confirmed by a bishop in another tradition, then all that is required is your public acceptance of the sufficiency of Anglican doctrine and worship and of your new bishop's authority. This is called Reception, usually by the bishop but sometimes by your parish priest acting on the bishop's behalf.

All this means that the process of becoming an Anglican is not so much a question of becoming a convert or of crossing a line, but more a case of being enveloped in a new way of life, a new way of seeing things. And the newness will be found in new assumptions and attitudes which creep up on you unnoticed, rather than in any strident banging of a newly acquired drum.

For this reason you will find many of us uneasy about the very term *Anglican* used as a description of a denominational group; much of the point of becoming an Anglican is that you are not a denomination but the Church of a country, no more, no less. In England noticeboards outside Anglican church buildings need only say "parish church," for no further description is necessary. Other Christian groups may feel the need to announce their separate identities with further adjectives. Anglicans do not. Although Anglicans from around the world may bridle at this innate Englishness (or perhaps we had better say Britishness for the sake of our good fellow-Anglicans in the rest of those islands), nevertheless this legacy of Englishness is something that binds us together around the world in our Anglican Communion of autonomous provinces.

In England, of course, Anglicanism is used to describe all that pertains to the Church of England, but here we are forced to recognize that the precise nature of the Church of England is as elusive as the nature of Englishness, or Britishness, itself.

Like Britain, which, though lacking a written constitution, has provided a model for democratic government for emergent nations across the world, so the Church of England, while lacking a definite "confession of faith" peculiar to itself, provides a model for the reunited Christian Church of the future; a Church in which disparate opinions and traditions are held together in creative tension and mutual love. The Church of England was never founded; like Topsy, it just grew, evolving slowly from a time nobody quite knows when, in a manner nobody quite knows how. Inevitably therefore, the "ism" of Anglicanism is misleading. It suggests a well-honed, coordinated system of belief, whereas what we have is more like a loose federation of churches, ideas, and attitudes, instinctive approaches and ways of doing things. All these elements cohere, fairly miraculously, into a quite distinctive way of life, easily recognizable and uncannily difficult to eradicate, at once both charming and infuriating.

Tied up as it is with the mysteries of Englishness, Anglicanism today runs the risk of being hijacked by the heritage industry and turned into a religious theme park. There are many today (on both sides of the Atlantic) who would have us major in quaintness. They would give the Church a leading role in a nostalgic trip down memory lane, rekindling folk-memories of cricket on the village green, warm beer, and ladies cycling to Evensong. Here is the quiescent, subservient Church, affectionately remembered, but kept in a drawer in the spare room, for special occasions only.

Not surprisingly, it is the land of Disney World that majors in the pursuit of the quaint. The Episcopal Church that has led the way on so many social and ecclesiastical issues steadfastly refuses to do so when it comes to worship. When its people assemble on the Lord's Day they (nearly) all climb into a time machine and go hurtling backward toward the good old days: a space-age ethic expressed in a stone-age worship.

But that would be to tell only part of the story. The Anglican *via media* may for some have the dynamism of a lugubrious worm, spineless and aimless, but it has proved itself to be a worm that turns. Now and again its bishops can become troublesome, whether Thomas Becket biting the royal hand that had fed him, or in recent times, Robert Runcie clipping the wings of Margaret Thatcher's jingoism after the Falklands conflict or Edmund Browning protesting outside the White House on the eve of the Gulf War, with an Episcopalian president in the Oval Office.

At the time of writing, the Anglican Communion faces the biggest-ever challenge to its unity and mutual charity as the biblical literalists challenge the Christian credentials of the open and progressive wing of our tradition. An international

WHERE DO WE GO FROM HERE?

commission headed by Archbishop Robin Eames is deliberating on how the Communion might continue, in the wake of Gene Robinson's consecration as Bishop of New Hampshire, to live with our differences in mutual respect and love. Meanwhile, although the vast majority of Anglicans are simply getting on with their lives, puzzled by all the fuss, ecclesiastical activists have worked themselves up into a state of frenzied excitement. The flash point may have been the ordination of gay men and women to the episcopate, but the issue boils down to one of authority.

Those who would use the Bible as an inerrant source of truth and as a weapon with which to beat others over the head are abandoning the deeply embedded Anglican understanding of Scripture, tradition, and reason as the three essential components that comprise our Christian formation. They would seek to replace this threefold basis of authority with Scripture only, and that has never been our way. Scripture is notoriously unreliable, and in fact unworkable, as a *sole* authority because of its total vulnerability to misguided or mischievous interpretation.

Going deeper still, the present crisis in the Anglican Communion reveals the fault line emerging right across mainstream Christianity, between a literal and a metaphoric understanding of the dogmas surrounding the person and purpose of Jesus the Christ, between the view that the book is closed once for all and that which says it is still being written.

To risk a gross over-simplification, the church in the northern hemisphere gave birth, in the era of unquestioned dogmas and unassailable truths, to a family that now peoples every corner of the world. Waking up to a different (post-Christian) world in Europe and North America, the church finds it now has less and less in common theologically with those of her offspring who still inhabit a world of utter certainty and combative evangelism. The kids have all the answers, while the parent has learned the hard way that life is full of questions.

Despite all this, we just about hold on. Perhaps the next few years will indeed see the disintegration of the Communion as we know it, but I somehow doubt it. There have been dire predictions before, during other times of crisis, and here we are still, having shed perhaps only a few extremists who weren't quite sure why they were with us anyway. And it's more than the Pension Fund that will cause us to think twice before jumping ship; it is above all those innate qualities of openness, generosity of spirit, and good humor that make us who we are.

We paddle along, rather than battle on, just occasionally surprising ourselves by getting something exactly right, and even producing a saint or two in the process (although we would never dream of saying so).

Setting down these few notes has prompted in me the most un-Anglican thought that I am, after all, rather *proud* to be an Anglican. I see just how often we *have* got it right, even though by accident rather than by design, and how good it is to breathe the fresh Anglican air. I have been reminded how richly blessed we are, and it would be good to think that something I have said may prompt you to come and share these blessings with us, and yourself become a blessing to enrich further our life together in this sometimes faltering but hopeful and quietly confident journey which is the Anglican approach to God.

> Father of all, we give you thanks and praise,
> that when we were still far off you met us in your
> Son and brought us home.
> Dying and living, he declared your love, gave us
> grace, and opened the gate of glory.
> May we who share Christ's body live his risen life;
> we who drink his cup bring life to others;
> we whom the Spirit lights give light to the world.
> Keep us firm in the hope you have set before us,
> so we and all your children shall be free,
> and the whole earth live to praise your name;
> through Christ our Lord.

Prayer after Communion
Common Worship 2000

 **Notes**

2. What's In a Name?

1   The Episcopal Church of the United States of America (ECUSA) is the official title of the Anglican Provinces within the United States.

2   Samuel Seabury (1729–96) was the first bishop of the Episcopal Church in the United States. Elected bishop in 1783, his consecration by English bishops was precluded by his inability to take the Oath of Allegiance to the Crown, the States having become independent. He was instead consecrated by Scottish bishops in Aberdeen on 14 November 1784.

3   David Jenkins, "God, Miracle and the Church of England," SCM Press, 1987.

3. To Begin at the Beginning

1   "The Church of England is part of the One, Holy, Catholic and Apostolic Church worshiping the one true God, Father, Son and Holy Spirit. It professes the faith uniquely revealed in the Holy Scriptures and set forth in the catholic creeds, which faith the Church is called upon to proclaim afresh in each generation." Words spoken by the bishop to a new parish priest in the Service of Institution and Induction, Diocese of Wakefield, United Kingdom.

2   The Supremacy of the Crown Act 1534. This legislation was repeated by Mary and toned down by Elizabeth I. Elizabeth's Act of Supremacy 1558 declared the Queen

to be "the only supreme governor of this realm, and of all her highness's dominions and countries, as well in all spiritual and ecclesiatical things or causes as temporal."

3   Cranmer's sister, Alice Cranmer, had been Prioress of Minster Abbey in Kent.

4   The work of translating the Bible into English began in the late fourteenth century, but did not gain the Church's backing until Miles Coverdale's version of 1535. Other versions followed, culminating in the Authorized Version of 1611, which remained the basic text until the twentieth century.

5   "Was this, then, a new Church or the old Church reformed and restored? If it is necessary, as Boniface VIII affirmed, for the salvation of every human creature that he should be subject to the Bishop of Rome, then the position of the Church of England is indefensible. But, if we look to Scripture, to the life of the early Church, to the great central tradition of the Church through all the centuries, we may come to think that the Church of England in the reign of Elizabeth I was right in claiming, as it claims today, that it and no other body is the Catholic Church in England." Stephen Neil, *Anglicanism*, Pelican, 1960, p. 132.

6   I have avoided use of the term *apostolic succession,* meaning "an unbroken succession of episcopal ordinations from the time of the apostles to the present day." This romantic notion cannot be proven by any church, only asserted, and gives far too much scope for the controversialists who love to spoil the picnic with accusations of broken chains or deficient intention.

Bearing in mind that controversialists on both sides can give as good as they get, and that there seems to be a fairly equal division of skeletons in cupboards, let's concentrate on continuity of *life*, with the *intention* of an unbroken line of commissioning through our bishops.

7   *Evangelical* in this context needs to be distinguished from *evangelistic. Evangelical* refers to a recognizable movement or party of like-minded individuals within the Church embracing the biblical faith outlined above. *Evangelistic* describes an attribute of the whole Church pertaining to our shared commission to be messengers of good news (*gospel* = *evangel*). While every Christian without exception therefore is called to be evangelistic, not every Christian will be an Evangelical.

8   "The elaboration of the Tractarian answer issued in a special theory of the Church of England, to which Newman gave the name of the *Via Media*." Geoffrey Faber, *Oxford Apostles*, Pelican, 1954, p. 324.

9   The term *Anglo-Catholic* is now rather dated.

10 Being rather hard of hearing, the Church of England managed to complete since the Second World War three major cathedrals—Liverpool, Coventry, and Guildford—which took not a scrap of notice of the Liturgical Movement and which as a result now look like beached whales.

11 ". . . the Church of England had shown plainly that it would not walk the way of either Geneva or Rome. This was the origin of the famous *Via Media*, the middle way, of the Church of England." Neil, p. 119.

4. Building Blocks: Essential Elements of Anglicanism

1 T. S. Eliot, "Four Quartets: Little Gidding" in *Complete Poems and Plays of T. S. Eliot*, Book Club Associates, 1977, p. 197.

2 "For my part, I travel not to go anywhere, but to go. I travel for travel's sake. The great affair is to move." Robert Louis Stevenson, *Travels with a Donkey*, Cheylard and Luc.

3 Fr. Raymond Raynes, Superior of the Community of the Resurrection, 1943 to 1958.

4 John Robinson (1919–83), bishop and theologian.

5 Jenkins, pp. 16–17.

5. From Chains to CD Rom: The Anglican Approach to Scripture

1 Jenkins, 81, p. 15.

2 "II Thess. was not meant to comment on I Thess. but to *displace* it." Gerd Ludemann, *Heretics*, SCM Press, 1996, p. 112.

3 "Most critics today reject the Petrine authorship." Introduction to the Letters to All Christians, 1966 edition of the *Jerusalem Bible*.

4 "What is there here beneath, better than fire, water, meats, drinks, metals of gold, silver, iron, and steel? Yet we see daily great harm and much mischief done by every one of these, as well for lack of wisdom and providence of them that suffer evil, as by malice of them that worketh evil . . . Wherefore I would advise you all, that cometh of the reading or hearing of this book, which is the word of God, the most precious jewel, and most holy relic that remaineth upon earth, that ye bring with you the fear of God, and that ye do it with all due reverence, and use your knowledge thereof, not to vainglory or frivolous disputation, but to the honour of God, increase of virtue, and edification both of yourselves and other." Thomas Cranmer, *Preface to the Great Bible* (Second Impression 1540).

5 Don't worry too much about which one you choose, as long as you end up with a version that makes sense of it for you. The Authorized (or King James) Version of 1611 continues to be sold, but it is not recommended that you start with this version.

6. Dogmas and Dugouts: The Anglican Approach to Doctrine

1   "There are no special Anglican doctrines, there is no particular Anglican theology. The Church of England is the Catholic Church in England. It teaches all the doctrines of the Catholic Faith, as these are to be found in Holy Scripture, as they are summarised in the ... Creeds, and as they are set forth in the decisions of the first four General Councils of the undivided Church." Neil, p. 417.

2   "Before working out in any way what is specifically Christian, it is important to stress just how much Christianity has in common with Judaism and Islam." Hans Küng, *Christianity*, SCM Press, 1995, p. 29.

3   John Julius Norwich, in his masterful account of the Eastern Empire, *Byzantium*, brilliantly portrays what the Council of Nicaea in 325 was really like: a strong-willed emperor determined to fix the outcome before the council began, a hopelessly unrepresentative body of bishops (7 from the West, 270 from the East), and participants mesmerized if not seduced by the wonders of Constantine's court, where (fugitives until yesterday) they now feasted in splendor. Norwich quotes Eusebius: "Detachments of the Emperor's personal guard and other troops surrounded the entrance to the palace with drawn swords, and through the midst of them the men of God proceeded without that fear into the innermost of the imperial apartments, in which some were the emperor's own companions at table, while others reclined on couches arranged on either side. One might have thought that a picture of Christ's kingdom was thus foreshadowed, and that the scene was less like reality than a dream" (Eusebius, *De Vita Constantini*, III, 15). John Julius Norwich, *Byzantium: The Early Centuries*, Penguin, 1990, p. 57.

4   Answer on being asked her opinion of Christ's presence in the Sacrament. S. Clarke, *Marrow of Ecclesiastical History*, 1675 edn, pt ii, *Life of Queen Elizabeth*.

5   The three post-apostolic doctrines decreed by Rome as necessary to salvation are: the Immaculate Conception of the Blessed Virgin Mary (1854); the Infallibility of the Pope (1870); and the Assumption of the Blessed Virgin Mary (1950).

6   Anglicans gain some wry amusement from the Vatican's horrified reaction to the Church of England's presumption in "going it alone" in ordaining women to the priesthood in 1994.

7   Recent examples are the Doctrine Commission's reports "We Believe in the Holy Spirit" (1991) and "The Mystery of Salvation" (1995).

8   The task is "to go on looking for the truth, with no reservations of any kind, to follow where love leads, to trust in life, to glory in the depth and the mystery, and not be afraid of what may be found in the depth and through the mystery." John Robinson quoted in Eric James, *John Robinson*.

9 "Do not seek orthodoxy, seek the truth." Abbé Huvelin quoted in Marvin O'Connell, *Critics on Trial*, CUA Press, 1994.

10 Ibid.

11 Dairmaid MacCulloch, *Thomas Cranmer*, Yale, 1996, p. 342.

7. Us and Me: The Anglican Approach to the Church

1 Fifty years ago, in contrast, local communities, in England and Wales at least, would have been divided by allegiance to either *church* or *chapel* (originating in the days when almost every village had a Methodist chapel as well as a parish church). Such distinctions are now almost obsolete: *church* is an acceptable word for every brand of Christianity, innocent of any particular theology or ecclesiology.

2 "A new stage in history calls for a new style of priesthood. What will its nature be? ... How are we to minister in today's culture, where formal religion is disregarded but spirituality is treasured?" Roderick Strange, Chairman of the National Conference of Priests, in *The Tablet*, 27 September 1997.

3 "Flagships of the Spirit," Platten and Lewis, 1998.

4 "It is hard to imagine any other institution which could have provided the solemnity and dignity required by the Princess of Wales' funeral ... Nowhere could have provided the vehicle for the overwhelming emotion and sense of the historic. At a point of national trauma, Westminster Abbey provided a reassuring sense of continuity." Madeleine Bunting in the *Guardian*, 13 September 1997.

5 "Cranmer came to hate the papacy, and therefore he needed the Royal Supremacy to fill the chasm of authority which had opened up in his thinking as a result ... in this he revealed a breathtaking scepticism about any independent character for the church." MacCulloch, *Thomas Cranmer*, pp. 15 and 78.

6 "The most spectacular single piece of iconoclasm so far in the English Church." Ibid., p. 227.

7 A recent example which gave heart to us all was the brave decision of President Mary McAleese (a Roman Catholic) to receive Holy Communion at an Anglican Eucharist in Christ Church Cathedral, Dublin, shortly after her Inauguration.

8. Bouquets and Bandages: The Anglican Approach to the Sacraments

1 "The open table fellowship of Jesus was thus perceived as a challenge to the purity system. And it was; the meals of Jesus embodied his alternative vision of an inclusive community." Marcus Borg, *Meeting Jesus Again for the First Time*, Harper, 1994, p. 56.

2 Preaching in 1547, Bishop Nicholas Ridley affirmed the Real Presence but discouraged all speculation about its nature. They were, he said, "worse than dogs and hogs, that would ask the question 'How he was there present?' " MacCulloch, p. 378.

3 "The art of ritual-making does not enslave, it frees. Ritual-making is an experience of liberation. Sadly, some people cannot tolerate the insecurity of freedom. Like the Israelites who complained to Moses in the desert, they prefer slavery." Gerard Pottebaum, *The Rites of People*, The Pastoral Press, 1992.

9. Decently and in Order: The Anglican Approach to Worship

1 "And the service itself [for Diana, Princess of Wales] was the Church of England at its undeniable best, supremely self-assured in its calm ceremony, pomp and quiet circumstance. It was nicely discreet about its Christianity for a plural society, welcoming and non-judgmental: the perfect recipe for an established Church on the verge of the millennium." Madeleine Bunting in the *Guardian*, 13 September 1997.

2 Colin Buchanan, *News of Liturgy*, June 1997.

3 Preface to the first Prayer Book (1549).

4 Gregory Dix, *The Shape of the Liturgy*, Dacre Press, 1945.

5 Preface to the first Prayer Book (1549).

6 The best place in all England in which to get the feel of all this is the tiny church at Little Gidding, Cambridgeshire, where in the seventeenth century a saint of a man called Nicholas Ferrar, a brilliant academic and a gifted MP, forsook the glittering prizes to hide himself away in rural obscurity to seek God and to gather around him a community of men and women. Utterly Anglican in spirit, the little community centered its life on the Divine Office recited daily in that beautiful and evocative place, hanging on gravely until the Civil War and the Puritan backlash finally engulfed them in 1646.

7 *Celebrating Common Prayer—A Version of the Daily Office SSF*, Mowbray, 1992.

8 Anglican Church Planting Initiatives, Bob and Mary Hopkins, 70 St. Thomas' Rd, Crookes, Sheffield S10 1UX, tel. 0114 267 8447, www.acpi.org.uk

9 Edward Schillebeeckx, OP, *God the Future of Man*, Sheed and Ward, 1968.

10. Learning Good Habits: The Anglican Approach to Prayer

1 *Opening Prayers*, Canterbury Press, 1999.

2 David Jenkins, *Still Living with Questions*, SCM Press, 1990.

3 Christopher Scott, *Between the Poles*, New Millennium, 1996.

4 Ibid.

5 "The Other," R. S. Thomas, *Collected Poems 1945–1990.*

6 Taizé Service, Norwich Cathedral, 29 November 1995.

11. Checks and Balances: The Anglican Approach to Authority

1 *Runcie: On Reflection,* compiled by Stephen Platten, Canterbury Press, 2002, p. 120.

2 It is generally agreed that the Pastoral Epistles—1 and 2 Timothy and Titus—although attributed to Paul, were written later by followers of his.

3 Set up after the Second World War to create complete new cities on green-field sites.

4 Various editions of the *Didache* are in circulation, one of which is included in Maxwell Staniforth, ed., *Early Christian Writings,* Penguin, 1968.

12. Loitering with Intent: The Anglican Approach to Membership

1 "It is lamentable that the vast majority of believers are confessing—not to say droning out—something every Sunday at worship which they no longer understand." Ludemann, *Heretics,* p. 190.

2 "Through them the individual Christian can enrol himself in the communion of all Christianity." Wolfgang Pannenberg, *The Apostles Creed in the Light of Today's Questions,* 1973.

3 "Religion is for me a journey of continual discovery in which I feel at home in the Church of England . . . The Anglican Church has encouraged me with the freedom to explore." Dame Cecily Saunders in *The Tablet,* 6 December 1997.

13. Seeing Both Sides: The Anglican Approach to Moral Questions

1 *Three Men in a Boat,* Jerome K. Jerome, 1889, Spring Books, 1977, p. 91.

2 Quoted in the *Dictionary of National Biography.*

3 1 Corinthians 9:27.

4 MacCulloch, op. cit., p. 58. Sadly, Cranmer toned down the original Sarum version of the wife's promise to be "bonner and buxom in bed and at the board."

5 *Liberal Evangelism,* Saxby, p 1.

14. Sending Us Out: The Anglican Approach to the Wider Community

1 "It is said that a third of the Cabinet are members of the Christian Socialist Movement." Clifford Longley in *The Tablet,* 19 July 1997.

2 "The concept of a God who suffers here and now, daily and hourly because it is the divine will to be involved forever with the sins and follies of mankind, was central to Studdert Kennedy's thought." William Purcell, *Woodbine Willie,* Hodder & Stoughton, 1962, p. 15.

3 Matthew 9:36.

4 Luke 8:21.

15. Taking a Lower Seat: The Anglican Approach to Other Traditions and Faiths

1 "If you are looking for a Catholic cook-book, the Two Fat Ladies, perhaps the most celebrated Catholics in Britain, have written again. It's not Catholic in content, so much as in spirit." Melanie McDonagh in *The Tablet,* 6 December 1997.

2 The bearers of the cross of Christ "slaughtered all the Muslims in the city and burnt all the Jews alive in the main synagogue." John Julius Norwich, *Byzantium: The Decline and Fall,* p. 42.

3 The Right Reverend Riah Abu El-Assal.

4 Among the many Anglican societies founded to promote overseas missionary work, the two most prominent were the Society for the Propagation of the Gospel (1701) and the Church Missionary Society (1799). In 1965, the former merged with the Universities' Mission to Central Africa (1857) to form the United Society for the Propagation of the Gospel.

5 James Boswell, *The Life of Samuel Johnson,* Penguin, 1986.

16. Where Do We Go from Here?

1 T. S. Eliot, "Four Quartets: Little Gidding" in *Complete Poems and Plays of T. S. Eliot,* Book Club Associates, 1977, p. 197.

2 Joseph Campbell, *The Hero with a Thousand Faces,* Princeton University Press, 1968, p. 25.